All rights reserved.

Thank you for purchasing an official copy of this book and for your copyright compliance.

No part of this publication may be reproduced, distributed, or transmitted in any form or by any means, including photocopying, recording, or other electronic or mechanical means, without the prior written permission of the publisher, except for short quotations in critical reviews and certain other non-commercial uses permitted by copyright law. Copyright infringement is a crime and can lead to civil and criminal liability.

info@cryptoz.media

DISCLAIMER

This book is intended solely for educational and informational purposes. The author and publisher do not provide financial advice, do not promote investment products, and do not guarantee any specific results from the application of the information contained in this publication. Trading in financial markets involves a high level of risk, including the possibility of losing all capital. Before you start trading, make sure that you are fully aware of all the risks and have a sufficient level of knowledge and experience. Neither the author nor the publisher is responsible for any loss or damage resulting from the use of information from this book. You make all financial decisions at your own risk.

info@cryptoz.media

FUNDAMENTALS OF TRADING

This chapter will lay the foundation for your trading training, focusing on the practical aspects and preparation for successful trading. We will rethink standard approaches, focusing on the key components needed to build an effective trading strategy.

1. UNDERSTANDING THE MARKET AND ITS PARTICIPANTS

To become a successful trader, understanding the market and its participants is paramount. The market is a complex system where each participant contributes to price formation and trading flows. Let's delve into the key aspects that will help you better understand market dynamics and make informed trading decisions.

DIVERSITY OF MARKET PARTICIPANTS

The market consists of a variety of different participants, each with their own objectives, strategies, and impact on price movem

THESE INCLUDE:

Retail Traders: Individual investors who trade in the market seeking profit. They may employ a wide range of strategies, from short-term scalping to long-term investments.

Institutional Investors: Banks, hedge funds, pension funds that trade in large volumes and can significantly influence market prices.

Market Makers: Firms or banks that offer to buy and sell an asset at a publicly quoted price, thereby providing market liquidity.

Algorithmic Traders: Participants who use automated systems to execute trading operations based on predefined algorithms and models.

IMPACT ON MARKET PRICES

Understanding how different types of participants interact in the market will help you better predict potential price movements. For example, large orders from institutional investors can cause significant price fluctuations, while market makers aim to maintain stability and liquidity in the market.

MARKET BEHAVIOR

Market behavior can vary significantly depending on current economic conditions, political events, and market sentiments. Understanding these factors

FUNDAMENTALS OF TRADING PSYCHOLOGY

Success in financial markets trading largely depends not only on knowledge and strategies but also on a trader's psychological resilience. Trading psychology plays a crucial role, helping manage emotions and behavior that can significantly impact trading outcomes. Let's delve deeper into how to control emotions, develop discipline and patience, and avoid common psychological traps.

MANAGING EMOTIONS

Emotional control is the first step towards successful trading. **The two primary emotions that need to be managed are:**

- **Fear:** Can lead to prematurely closing profitable positions out of fear of losing gains or refraining from opening new positions due to the fear of losses.

- **Greed:** Encourages traders to risk too much or hold onto positions for too long in hopes of even higher profits.

To manage these emotions, it's essential to understand that trading is a game of probabilities, and every trade has both the potential for profit and the risk of loss. Establishing clear rules for entering and exiting trades can help mitigate emotional impact.

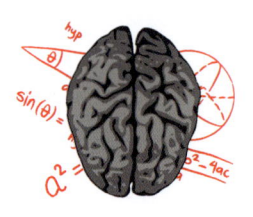

DEVELOPING DISCIPLINE AND PATIENCE

Discipline and patience are necessary to follow your trading strategy even in times of market uncertainty.

This includes:

- **Adhering to a trading plan:** Not deviating from pre-set rules, even if intuition suggests otherwise.

- **Patiently waiting for the right market conditions:** Not trading for the sake of trading, but waiting for ideal conditions for your strategies.

AVOIDING PSYCHOLOGICAL TRAPS

There are several common psychological traps that are easy to fall into:

- **Overconfidence effect:** Overestimating one's trading skills after a series of successful trades can lead to excessive risks.

- **Confirmation bias:** Seeking information that confirms your prior beliefs while ignoring signals that suggest the contrary.

- **Hindsight bias:** Believing that past events could have been predicted and used for profit, which can lead to unrealistic expectations from trading.

DEVELOPING EMOTIONAL RESILIENCE

To develop emotional resilience, it's beneficial to practice meditation and mindfulness techniques. These can help maintain a clear mind and reduce the impact of stress and emotions on decision-making.

③ DEVELOPING A TRADING STRATEGY

Reating an effective trading strategy is a fundamental aspect that defines your success in the financial markets. A well-thought-out strategy not only aids in making informed decisions but also in managing risks. Let's take a closer look at the key steps in developing your trading strategy.

DEFINING TRADING GOALS

Before embarking on strategy development, it's crucial to clearly define your trading goals. These could be daily, weekly, or monthly profitability targets, acceptable risk levels, long-term investment goals, and so on. Goals should be realistic and measurable to assess the effectiveness of your strategy.

CHOOSING A TRADING STYLE

The choice of trading style depends on your temperament, available time for trading, and the level of risk you're willing to tolerate.

TRADING STYLES INCLUDE

- **Long-term Trading (Positional):** Suitable for those willing to hold assets for many months or even years, awaiting significant market changes.

- **Swing Trading:** Focuses on capturing 'swings' or market movements that can last from several days to several weeks.

- **Day Trading:** Involves entering and exiting trades within a single trading day, avoiding holding positions open overnight.

- **Scalping:** A short-term trading strategy where traders aim to profit from small price changes, making numerous trades throughout the day.

DEVELOPING ENTRY AND EXIT CRITERIA

Define clear conditions under which you will enter and exit a trade. This may include specific chart patterns, technical analysis indicators, support and resistance levels, or economic indicators. It's also important to determine how you will set stop-losses and take-profits to manage risks.

TESTING THE STRATEGY ON HISTORICAL DATA

Before applying the strategy in live trading, it's important to test it on historical data. This will help you understand how your strategy might have performed under different market conditions and allow you to make necessary adjustments. Using backtesting software can significantly simplify this process.

CONTINUOUS LEARNING AND ADAPTATION

Markets are constantly changing, so your strategy should be adaptive as well. Regularly analyze the performance of your strategy and be ready to make changes based on new data and market conditions. Continuous learning and adaptation are key to long-term trading success.

Developing a trading strategy is an iterative process that requires time, patience, and continuous self-improvement. By following these recommendations, you can create a solid foundation for your trading career.

EXPLORING TRADING STRATEGIES

① WHEN TO TRADE AND WHEN TO HOLD

In this chapter, we will dive deep into trading strategies, a crucial element for successful trading. Making the decision on when to enter the market or, conversely, to refrain from trading requires a deep understanding of market conditions and self-discipline. This choice should be based on strategic analysis and alignment with your personal trading plan. Let's look in detail at the key aspects that will help you make an informed decision.

ANALYZING MARKET CONDITIONS

Before deciding whether to enter the market, it's essential to conduct a thorough analysis of market conditions, which includes:

- **Trends:** Identifying the overall direction of the market can help you understand whether the market is in an upward trend, downward trend, or moving sideways.

- **Volatility:** High volatility can offer great opportunities for profit but also comes with high risk. It's important to assess whether the current level of volatility matches your risk appetite.

- **Economic Indicators and News:** Events such as the release of economic reports or significant political announcements can significantly impact market prices. Being informed about upcoming events will help you make a decision about trading.

ADHERENCE TO YOUR TRADING PLAN

Your trading plan should include clear criteria for entering and exiting the market. Before making a decision to trade, ensure that the current market conditions meet these criteria. Resist the temptation to enter the market without a clear signal from your strategy.

RISK MANAGEMENT

Recognizing and managing risks is a key aspect of making trading decisions. Determine the maximum level of risk you are willing to accept for a trade, and do not exceed it. Using stop-loss orders can help limit potential losses.

PSYCHOLOGICAL PREPARATION

Trading requires not only analytical skills but also psychological resilience. Ensure that you are in the correct emotional state before making a trading decision. Avoid trading under the influence of emotions such as fear or greed.

TIMING HOLDS

The decision to hold can be as important as the decision to enter the market. If market conditions have changed and no longer align with your strategy, or if you have reached your profit target, it may be wise to close the position. It's also important to review your open positions to ensure they still align with your risk management plan.

2 THE ROLE OF TECHNICAL ANALYSIS

Technical analysis plays a central role in trading strategies, providing traders with tools to analyze market prices and trends without considering fundamental factors such as news and economic indicators. It's based on the study of price charts and trading volumes with the aim of predicting future market movements. Let's examine the key aspects and principles of technical analysis in detail.

HISTORY REPEATS ITSELF

The fundamental premise of technical analysis is that market behavior tends to repeat itself. This means that certain patterns and chart formations observed in the past can give insights into future price movements. Traders use this data to identify potential entry and exit points in the market.

TREND ANALYSIS

Identifying the trend is a key task in technical analysis. Trends can be upward, downward, or sideways, and they indicate the general direction of price movement. Traders aim to trade in the direction of the trend since "the trend is your friend." Tools such as moving averages help determine the current trend and potential changes in direction.

SUPPORT AND RESISTANCE LEVELS

Support and resistance levels are critically important concepts in technical analysis. A support level is a price level below which the price of an asset typically does not fall, while a resistance level is a level above which the price does not usually rise. Traders use these levels to identify potential price reversal points and moments to open or close positions.

TECHNICAL INDICATORS

Technical indicators are mathematical calculations based on price and/or trading volumes that help traders identify trends, momentum, and other market characteristics. There are numerous indicators, including moving averages, the Relative Strength Index (RSI), MACD, and the stochastic oscillator. Each indicator provides unique information about market conditions and can be used in combination to refine trading signals

CHART PATTERNS

Chart patterns, such as head and shoulders, double tops and bottoms, flags, and triangles, represent specific shapes on the price chart that can indicate a continuation or reversal of the current trend. Studying these patterns allows traders to predict future price movements and make informed trading decisions.

THE IMPORTANCE OF TESTING

Before applying technical analysis in real trading, it's important to test strategies on historical data. This helps determine the effectiveness of certain indicators and patterns under various market conditions.

Technical analysis is a powerful tool in a trader's arsenal, allowing not only to predict future price movements but also to manage risks through informed trading decisions. However, it's important to remember that no tool or method of analysis can guarantee 100% success, so it's vital to use technical analysis in conjunction with other strategies and careful risk management.

CHART PATTERNS CHEAT SHEET

Double Top
- Neckline
- Stop
- SELL/SHORT
- Target

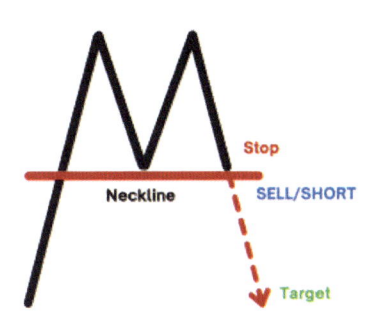

Head & Shoulders
- Neckline
- Stop
- SELL/SHORT
- Target

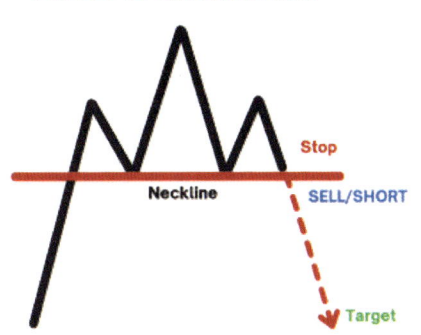

Inverse Head & Shoulders
- Neckline
- Target
- BUY/LONG

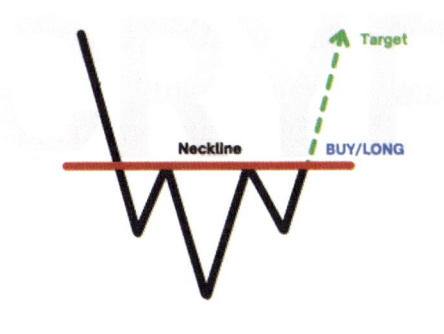

Double Bottom
- Neckline
- Target
- BUY/LONG
- Stop

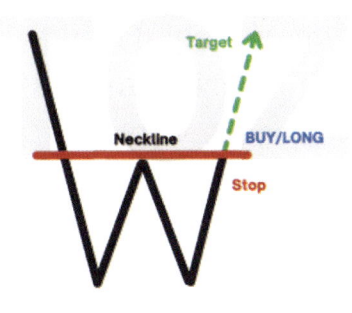

Rising Wedge
- Stop
- SELL/SHORT
- Target

Bullish Pennant
- Target
- BUY/LONG
- Stop

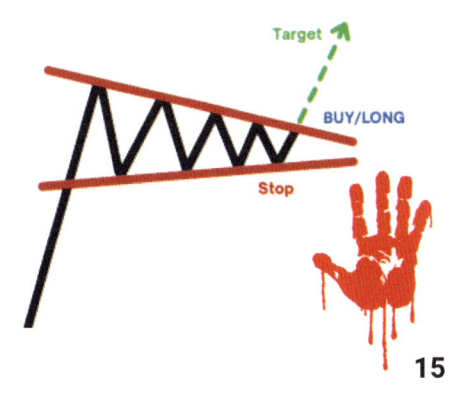

Falling Wedge

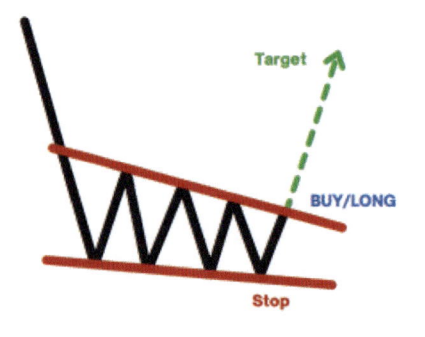

Bullish Rectangle

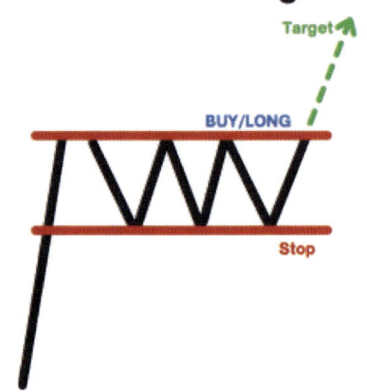

Descending Triangle

Rising Wedge

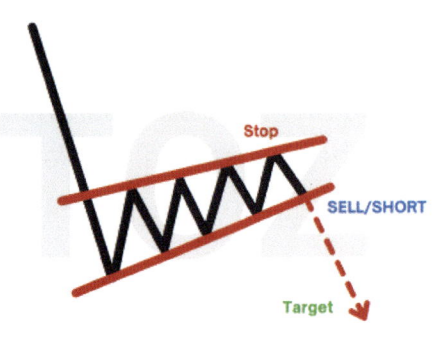

Symmetrical Triangle

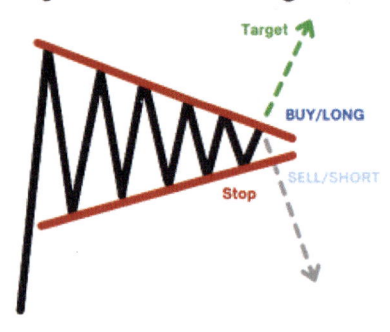

Falling Wedge

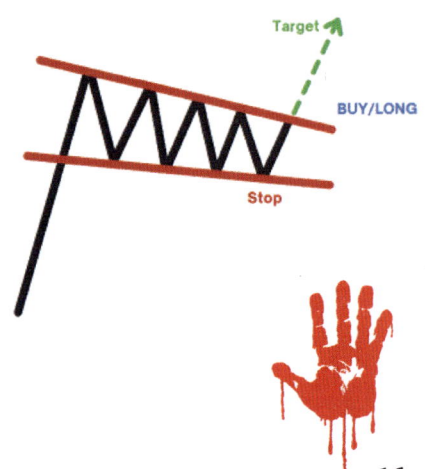

Flag

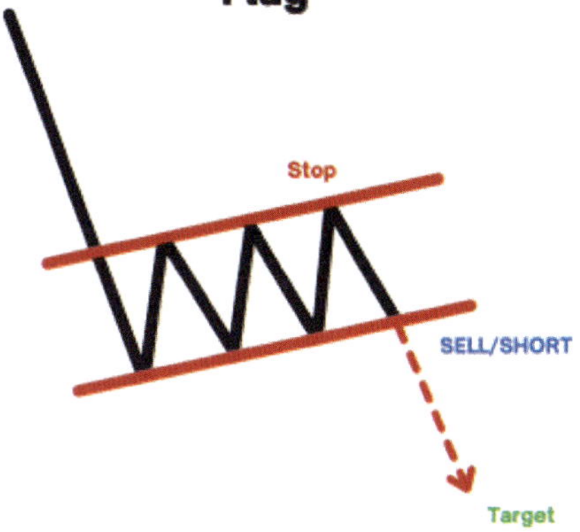

Bearish Pennant

Flag

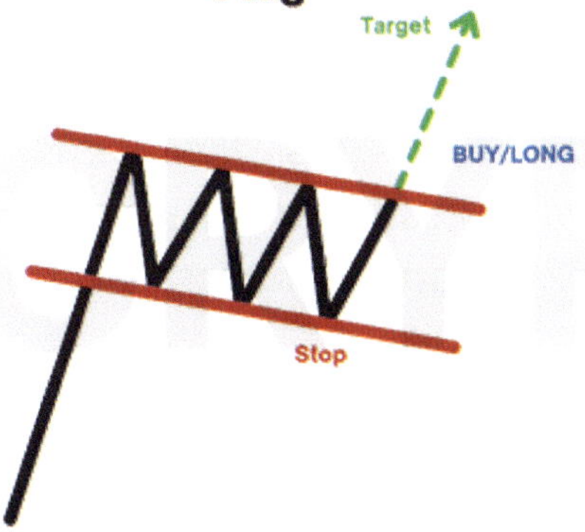

Symmetrical Triangle

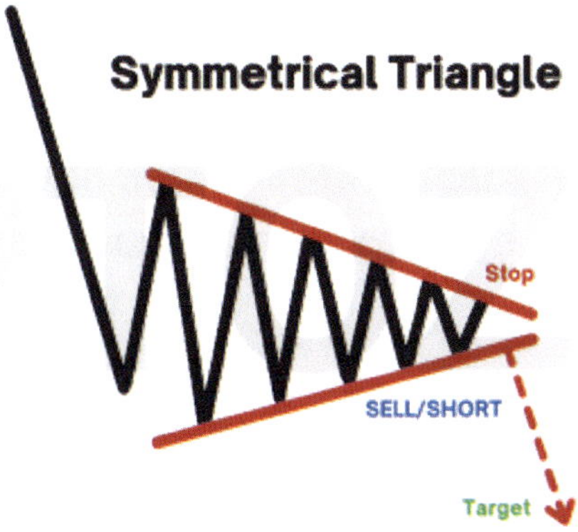

Ascending Scallop

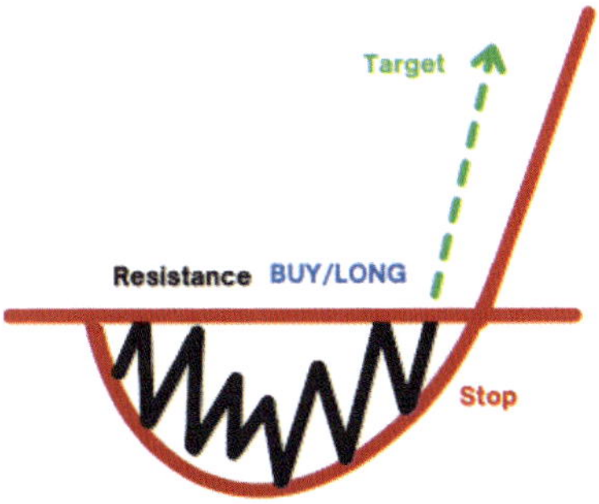

Ascending Triangle

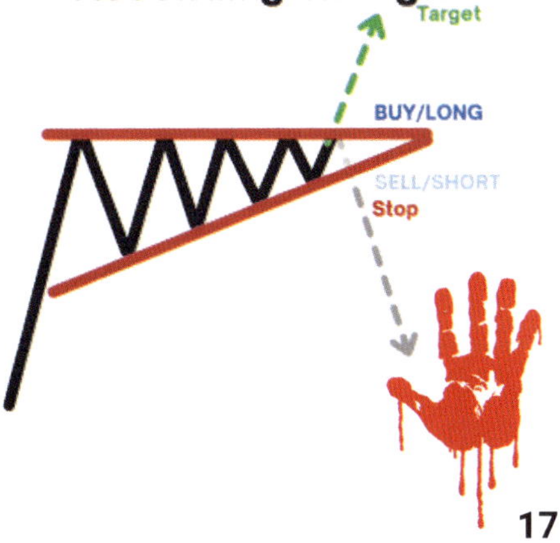

TRADING PRICE ACTION PATTERNS & SUPPORT & RESISTANCE ZONES

This is a full "Anatomy" behind trading patterns. Always looking for these timeframes for trading patterns and support/resistance (supply/demand) zones to get a better confirmation:

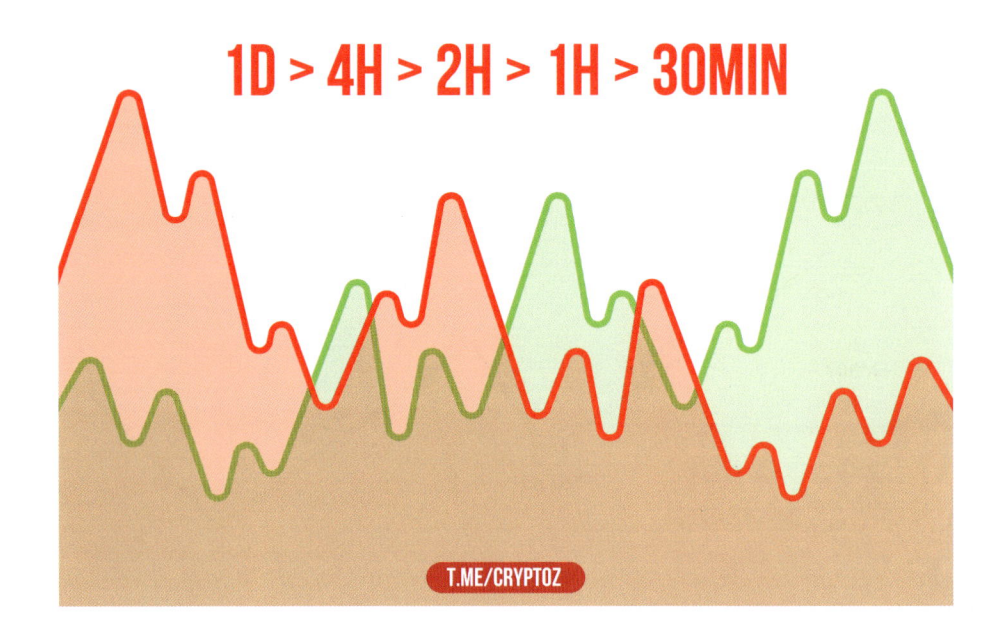

1D > 4H > 2H > 1H > 30MIN

T.ME/CRYPTOZ

BUMP AND RUN PATTERN

- The initial stage of the bump-and-run chart pattern is the lead-in phase, characterized by a consistent price increase without excessive speculation.
- For a valid bump and run trading pattern, the trend line should slope upward between 30 to 45 degrees.
- The lead-in trend line serves as either a support or resistance level, depending on the market.
- It is instrumental in identifying the entry point when the market changes direction during the run-up phase.
- The bump phase kicks off with a sudden spike in price owing to heightened speculative activity.
- The final phase commences when the price retraces back to the crucial support or resistance level.
- Typically, prices rebound from this level at least twice before resuming the trend's direction.
- Opening a short position post the figure's breakout is crucial.
- Target refers to the level where you intend to close an open trade.

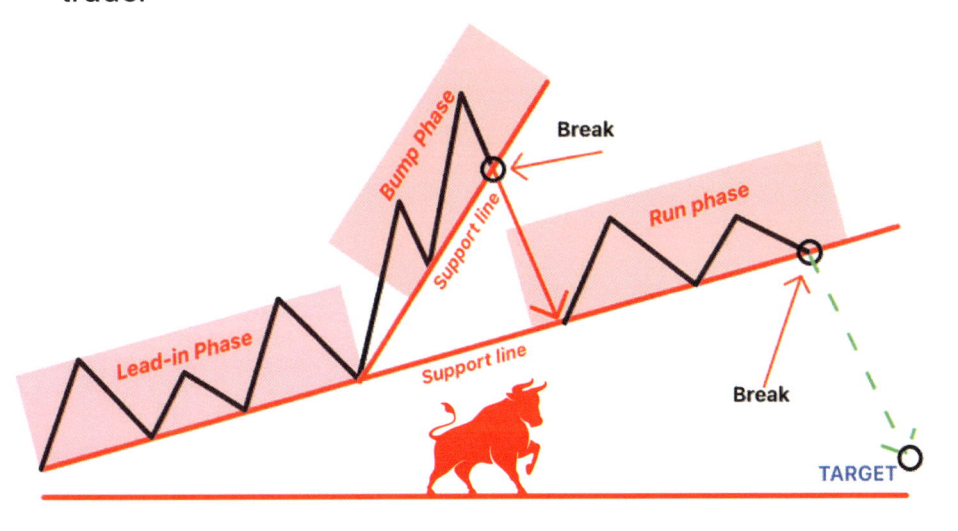

BUMP AND RUN REVERSAL PATTERN

- The initial stage of the bump-and-run chart pattern is the lead-in phase, characterized by a consistent decline in price without excessive speculation.
- For a valid bump-and-run trading pattern, the trend line should slope downward at approximately 30 to 45 degrees.
- The lead-in trend line serves as a support or resistance level depending on market conditions and helps determine the entry point for trading when the market changes direction during the run-up phase.
- The bump phase commences with a rapid price spike caused by increased speculative activity.
- The final phase occurs when the price retraces to the critical support or resistance level.
- Typically, prices rebound from this level at least twice before continuing in the trend's direction.
- To capitalize on the pattern, it is essential to initiate a long position after the breakout occurs. Set a target for closing the trade at the desired level.

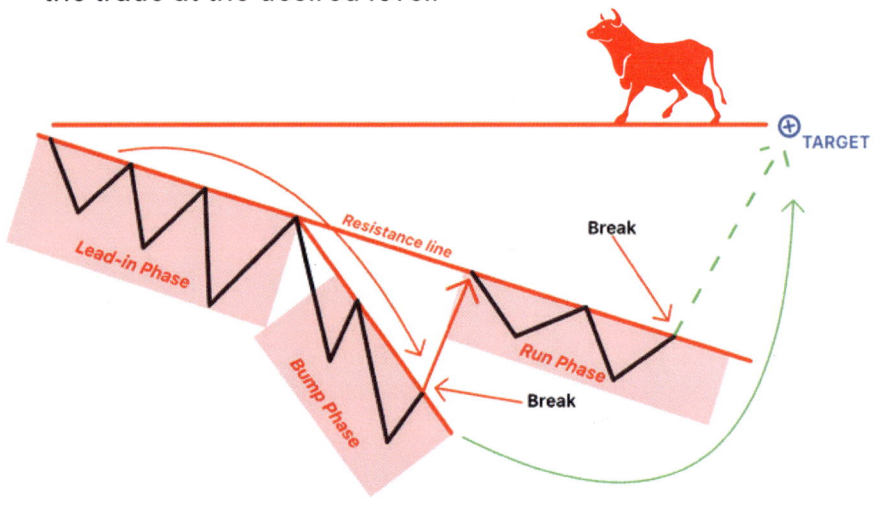

BULISH PATTERN "WOLFE WAVE"

The Wolf pattern essentially unfolds as an expanding wedge, marked by a sequence of rising and falling points, initiating with point 1, the precursor to the initial peak in a bullish setup. "Base" aptly describes this starting point, indicating a trio of consecutive extremal points - 2, 3, and 4. Point 1 often emerges amidst market consolidation.

Point 2 acts as the foundation for the initial apex. Following this, point 3 represents the lowest price in the correction phase post the first peak (point 2).
Point 4 reaches the zenith of the second apex.
Point 1, preceding point 2 (the peak), surpasses point 3 (the correction).
Point 5 marks the entry spot (where ray 1-3 intersects).
Point 6, the peak* (profit realization point), is determined by the crossing of the price trajectory with ray 1-4.

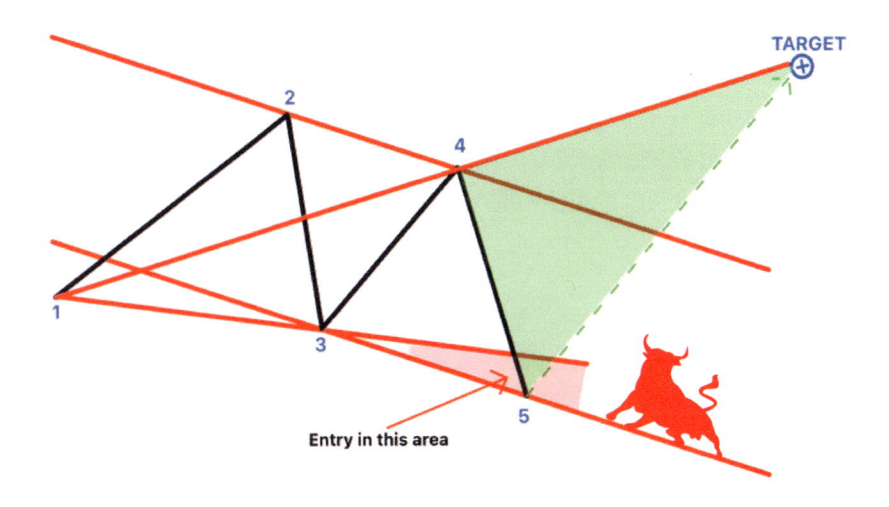

BEARISH PATTERN " WOLFE WAVE"

The Wolf pattern essentially manifests as an expanding wedge, characterized by a succession of progressive highs and lows beginning at point 1. This initial point, termed the base, precedes the bullish pattern's first peak, signifying a pivotal line connecting three successive extremal points—either maximum or minimum price values—identified as points 2, 3, and 4. Point 1 may be formed during consolidation.

Point 2 marks the foundation of the initial correction, while point 3 represents the peak price following this correction.
Point 1 serves as the initial base leading up to point 2, the first correction, without surpassing point 3. Conversely.
Point 4 denotes the nadir following the second peak.
Point 5 is defined as the entry point, occurring at the intersection of rays 1-3, termed the Sweet Zone.
Finally, point 6 signifies the culmination or the profit-taking point, identified by the price chart's intersection with ray 1-4.

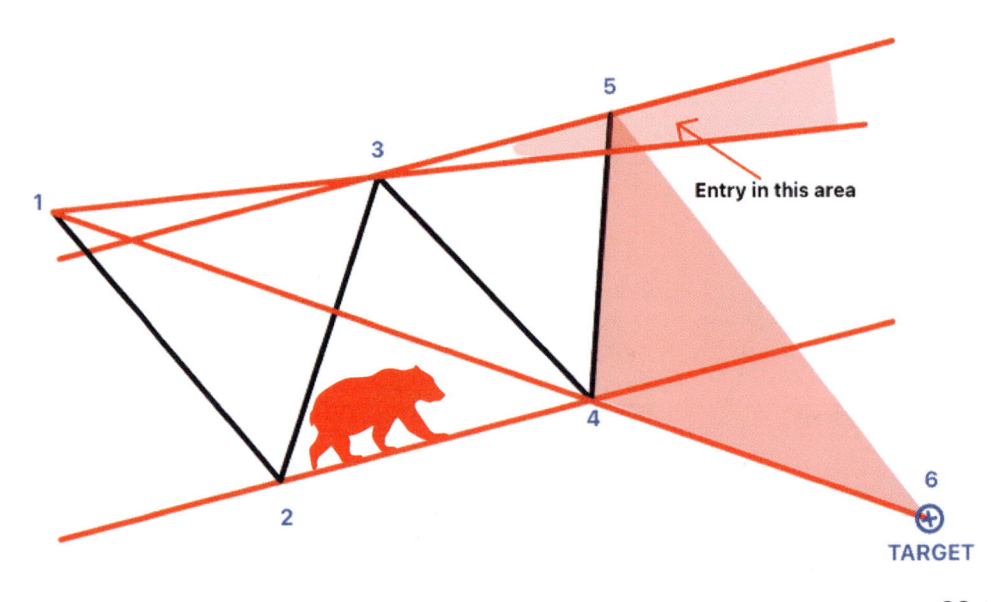

DOUBLE BOTTOM

- This pattern suggests that the downtrend is nearing its end, indicating strong momentum from buyers and a reluctance from sellers to hold their positions.

- The initial bottom represents the local minimum and the lowest point within the current trend, serving as the starting point for the support line.

- The second bottom emerges after a retracement with typically lower trading volume. Typically, this second bottom validates the support line.

- Two entry options are available for initiating a position.
- TARGET: the desired point to close an open position!

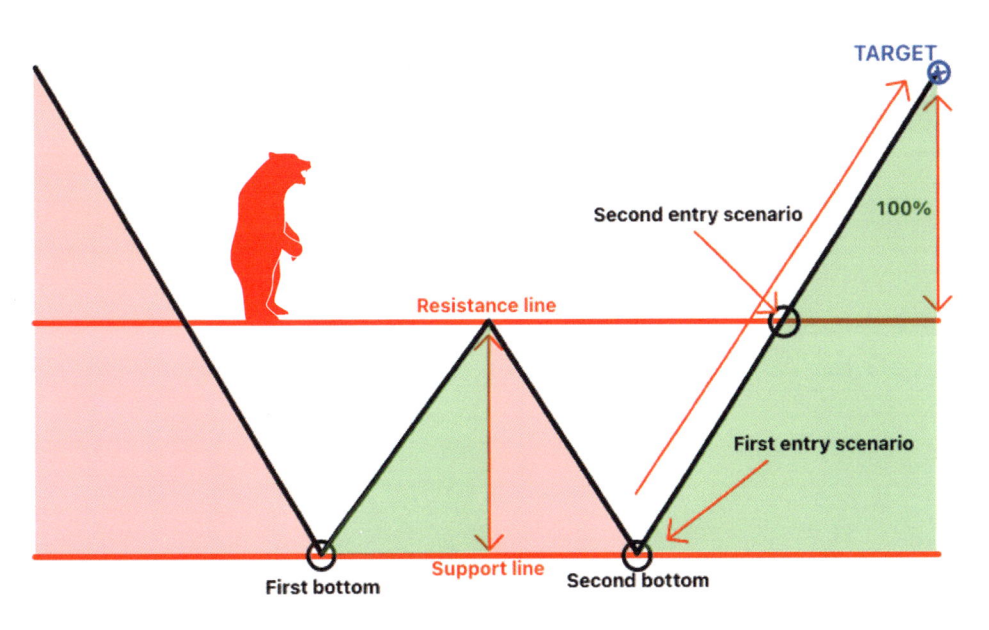

DOUBLE TOP

- The emergence of this pattern signals the conclusion of an uptrend, indicating strong selling pressure and buyers relinquishing their positions.

- The initial peak represents the local maximum and the highest point in the ongoing trend, marking the commencement of the support line.

- Following a retracement, the second peak is typically characterized by reduced trading volume and typically validates the support line.

- Two entry options are available for initiating a position.
- TARGET - (the designated point for closing an open position)

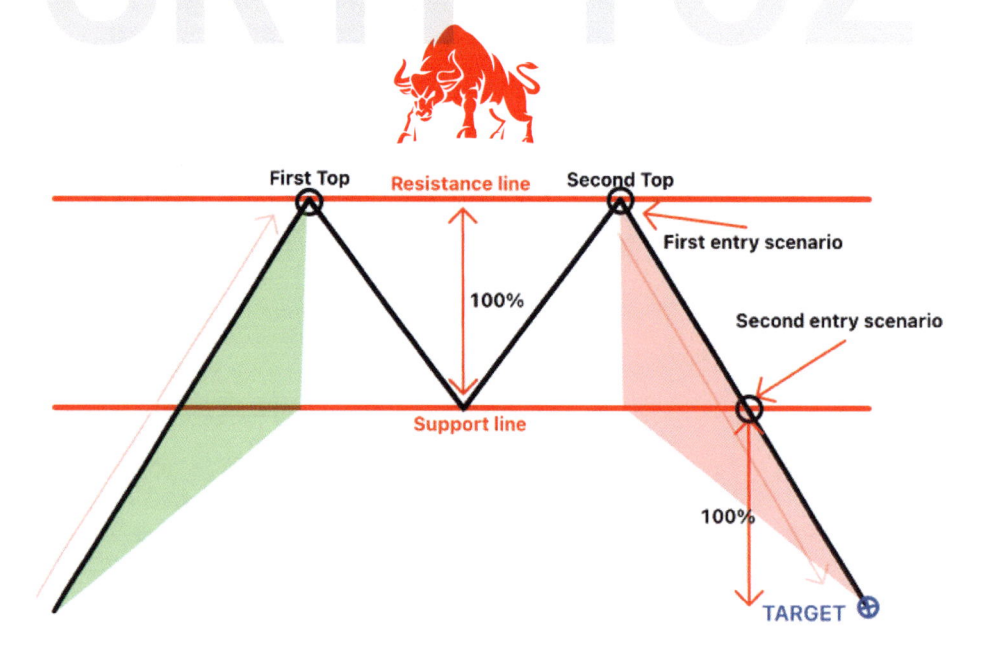

TRIPLE BOTTOM

The downtrend is crucial for the development of the "Triple Bottom" pattern. The longer it lasts, the more reliable the signal becomes for this pattern to take shape.

- Three lows should create a distinct support line.

- Trading volume typically decreases during the pattern formation, but there could be spikes in volume at the peaks, although each peak may have less volume.

- Confirmation of the pattern occurs only after breaking the resistance line (neckline).

- Two entry options are available for opening a position.
- TARGET - (the level at which you aim to close an open position)

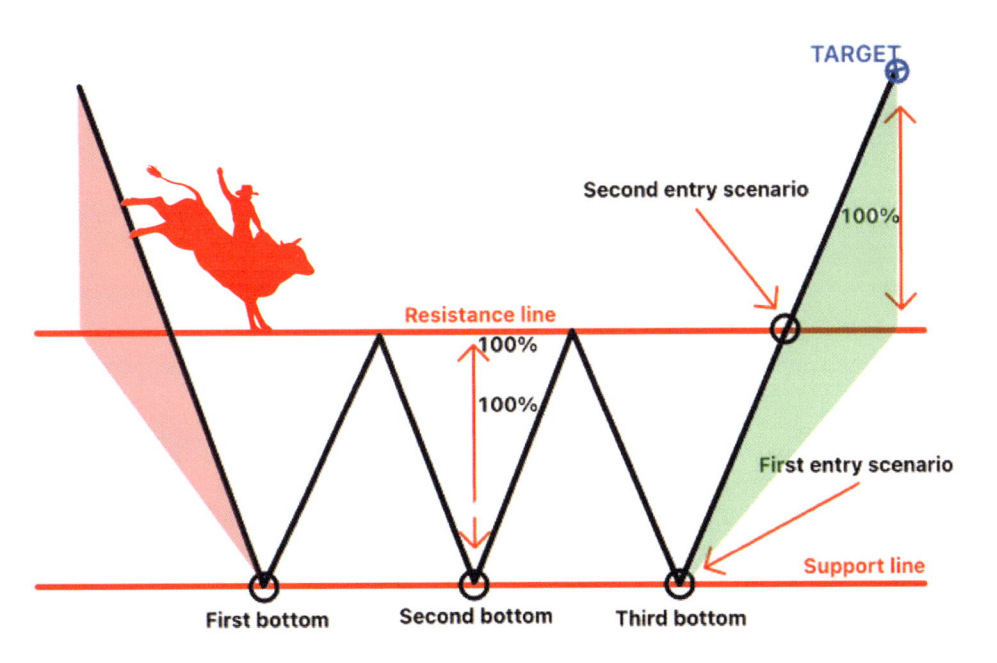

TRIPLE TOP

An uptrend is essential for the development of the "Triple Top" pattern. The longer the uptrend lasts, the more dependable the signal for this pattern becomes.

- The three peaks need to create a distinct resistance line, typically at the same resistance level. Clear bottoms between the peaks should form a solid support line, possibly with small shadows on the support.

- Generally, the trading volume decreases while the pattern forms, but there could be an increase in volume at the peaks. However, the volume tends to decrease with each subsequent peak.

- Two entry options are available for opening a position.
- TARGET: The desired closing point for an open position.

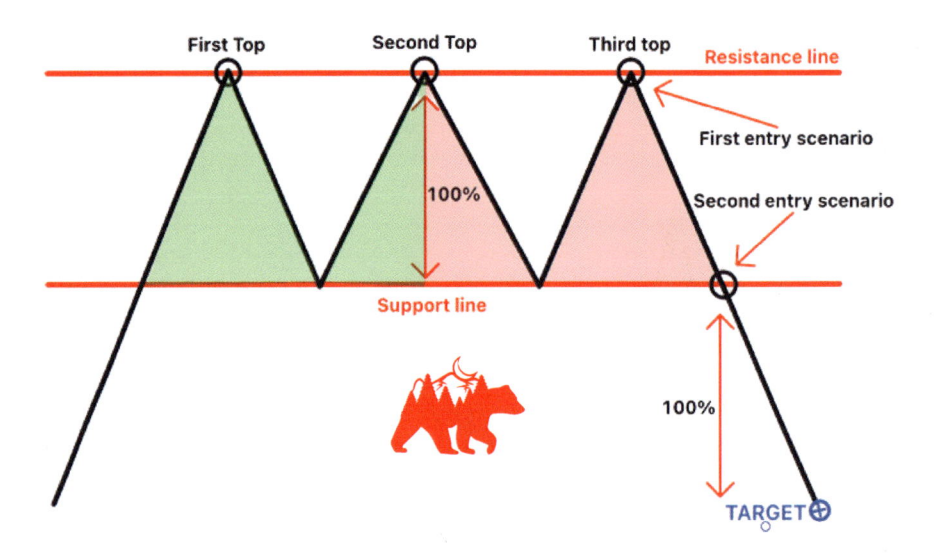

HEAD AND SHOULDERS

- The peak at the left shoulder signifies the peak of the ongoing uptrend. The subsequent price decrease finalizes the creation of the first shoulder.

- The head begins at the initial low point. The price increase lifts the head above the prior peak (left shoulder), establishing a new peak.

- The right shoulder emerges following the second low point. Positioned below the central peak (head), the right shoulder aligns with the level of the left shoulder.

- Two entry options are available for initiating a position.
- TARGET - (the designated point for closing an open position!)

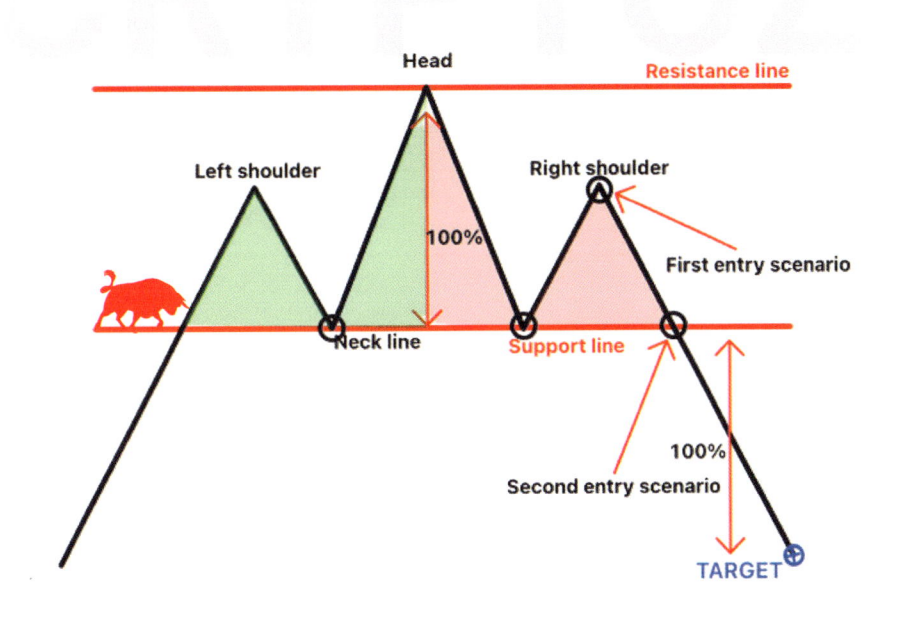

BEARISH HEAD AND SHOULDERS

- A bearish head and shoulders pattern typically follows a significant downtrend before its completion.

- The formation of the left shoulder occurs when the downtrend hits a new historical low, followed by a correction.

- After the price correction of the left shoulder, there is a decline leading to a new low. The subsequent price correction forms the head, with its peak being the second point used to create the neckline.

- Two entry options are available for opening a position.
- TARGET: the desired closing point for an open position.

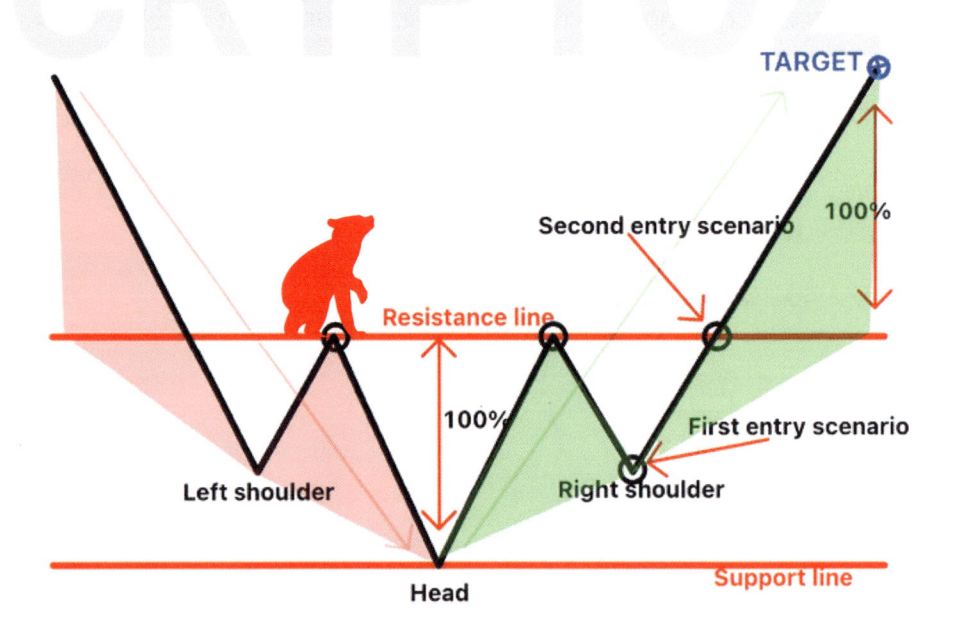

DRAGON PATTERN

- To form the Dragon pattern, a trend line must be drawn through the head and hump of this model ("Ridge of the Dragon").

- The Dragon's head represents the highest price point of the pattern, while the first paw indicates the local price minimum.

- The Dragon's hump signifies the peak price between its paws.

- The second paw of the Dragon indicates another minimum position, slightly below or above the first paw, and rarely equal to it.

- To enter a position, wait for the trend line to be broken.

- The Tail of the Dragon marks the target price that will yield profits.

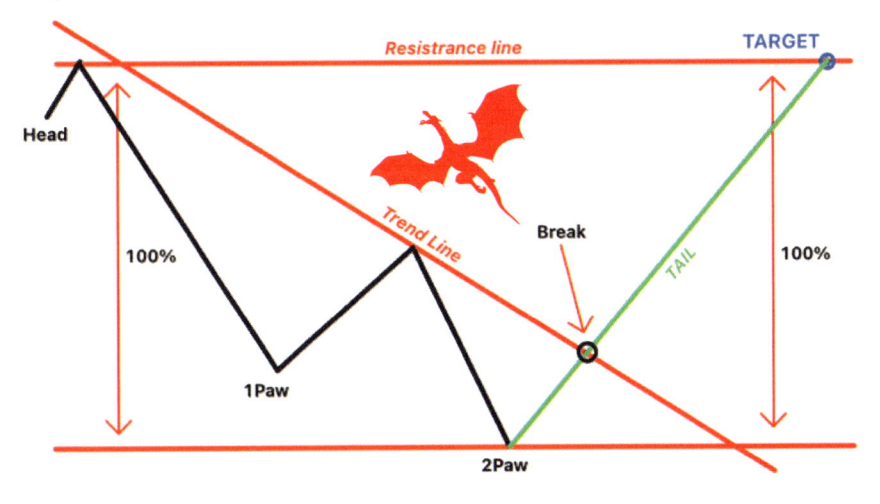

DRAGON BEARISH PATTERN

For the Dragon formation, a trend line should be drawn through the head and hump of the model ("Ridge of the Dragon").

- Dragon head: represents the lowest price point of the figure.

- The first paw of the Dragon: denotes a local price peak.

- Dragon's hump: signifies the lowest price between its paws..

- The second paw of the Dragon: another peak, usually slightly below the first paw, and in some cases, equal to the first paw's peak.

- Position should be opened after the trendline is broken.

- The Tail of the Dragon: a target price to achieve income.

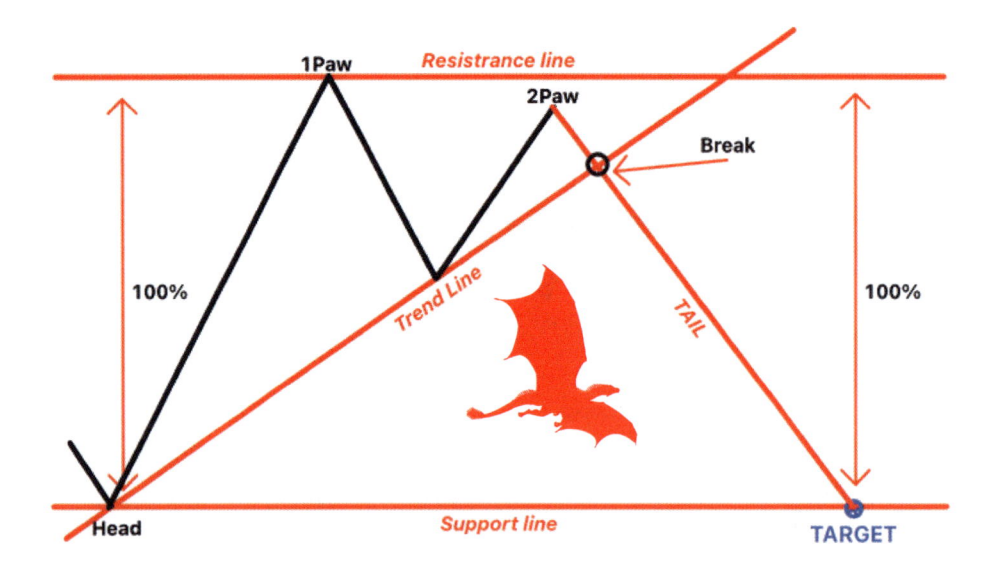

PATTERN "ASCENDING SCALOP"

"The "Scallop" pattern trading strategy operates in the following manner: consider initiating a long position when prices surpass the resistance level.

The optimal entry point for your purchase order is slightly above the breakout point. However, ensure that the breakout candle closes above the resistance line.

"Bowl" patterns indicate long-term reversal patterns, while "Scallop" patterns suggest short-term continuation patterns.

- It is essential to open a long position following the pattern break.

- Target refers to the point where you intend to close an open trade."

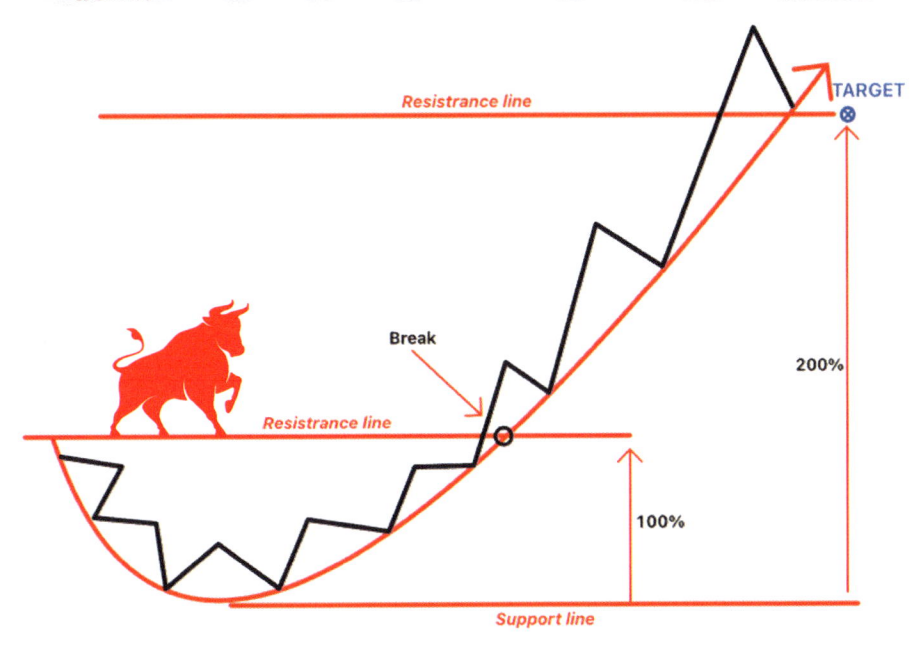

PATTERN "DESCENDING SCALOP"

"The "Scallop" pattern trading strategy operates in the following manner: consider initiating a short position when prices surpass the resistance level.

The optimal entry point for your purchase order is slightly above the breakout point. However, ensure that the breakout candle closes above the resistance line.

"Bowl" patterns indicate long-term reversal patterns, while "Scallop" patterns suggest short-term continuation patterns.

- It is essential to open a long position following the pattern break.

- Target refers to the point where you intend to close an open trade."

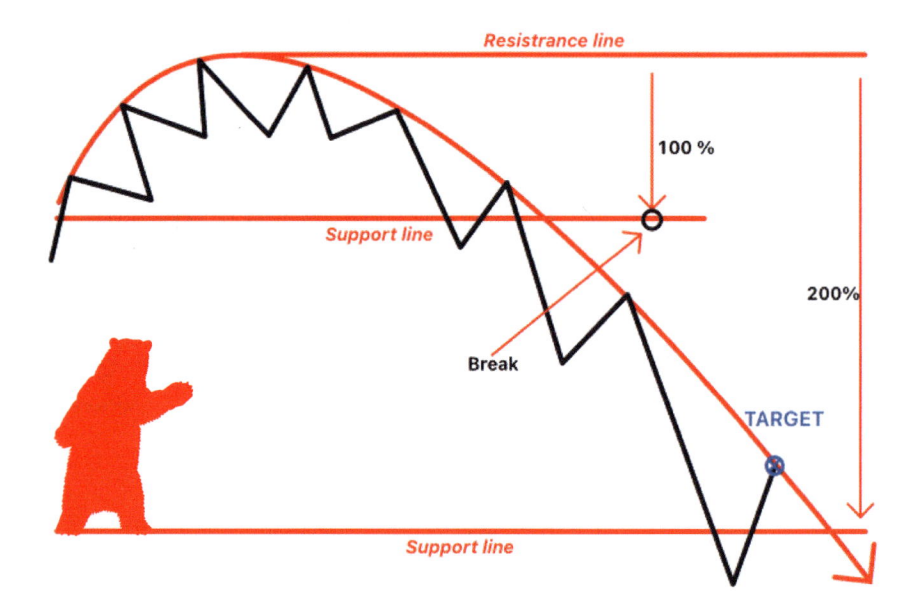

PATTERN "CUP"

- The cup pattern is relatively rare but highly dependable when it comes to bullish trends. Typically, it emerges at the conclusion of a long-term bearish market movement, signaling a potential market reversal.

- A descending price trend with a gradual slowdown. In its classic form, it should create a smooth arc.

- In simple terms, a rounded bottom depicts a scenario where major market players hold positions, making it challenging for prices to fall further. Once this resistance is overcome, phase 3 of the formation – the growth phase – commences.

- Price increase - a rise that ideally mirrors the earlier downtrend in duration, forming a symmetrical pattern. This phase is characterized by a gradual acceleration in price growth.

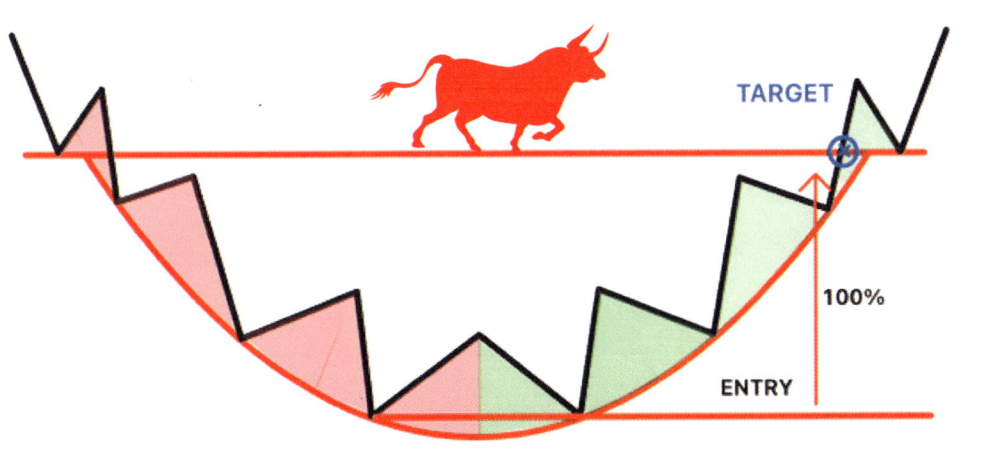

PATTERN "BEARISH CUP"

The "Inverted Cup" serves as a relatively uncommon yet highly dependable bearish pattern. Typically emerging at the conclusion of an extended bullish trend, it often indicates an upcoming market reversal.

- Prices show an upward trend with a gradual deceleration. Ideally, this phase should form a smooth arc in the classical scenario.

- A rounded bottom signifies a massive sell-off by major market players, indicating a struggle to maintain price levels. Once this becomes unsustainable, phase 3 of the formation initiates (i.e., the fall).

- The price decline after reaching its peak should be viewed as the entry point, lasting a duration similar to the initial ascending phase.

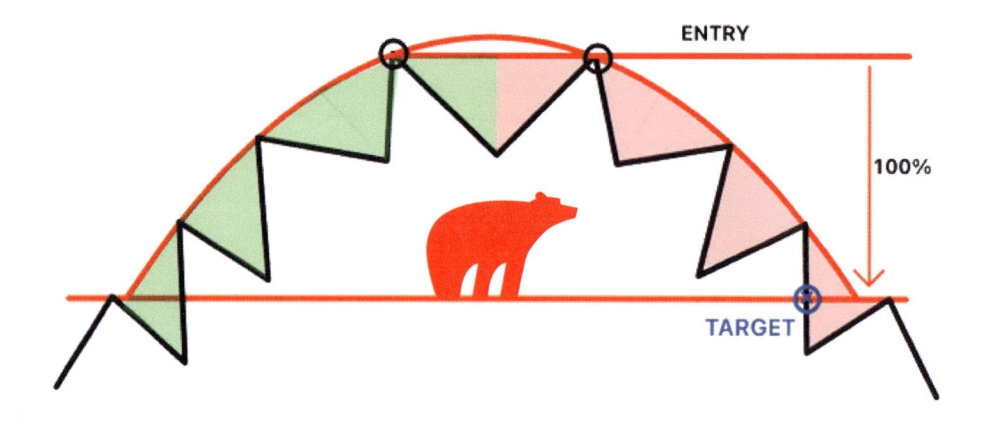

PATTERN "DIAMOND"

- The formation of the pattern occurs on higher timeframes (approximately 1 hour). A stronger indication of a reversal is presented with longer timeframes.

- The more evident and enduring a trend is in the market, the greater the impact of the pattern on the reversal.

- Additionally, if significant candles with minimal shadows break one side of the during the pattern formation, it reinforces the pattern's strength.

- Confirming the likelihood of the pattern forming and playing out, pullbacks within the correction corridor aligning with previously tested crucial support/resistance levels is also significant.

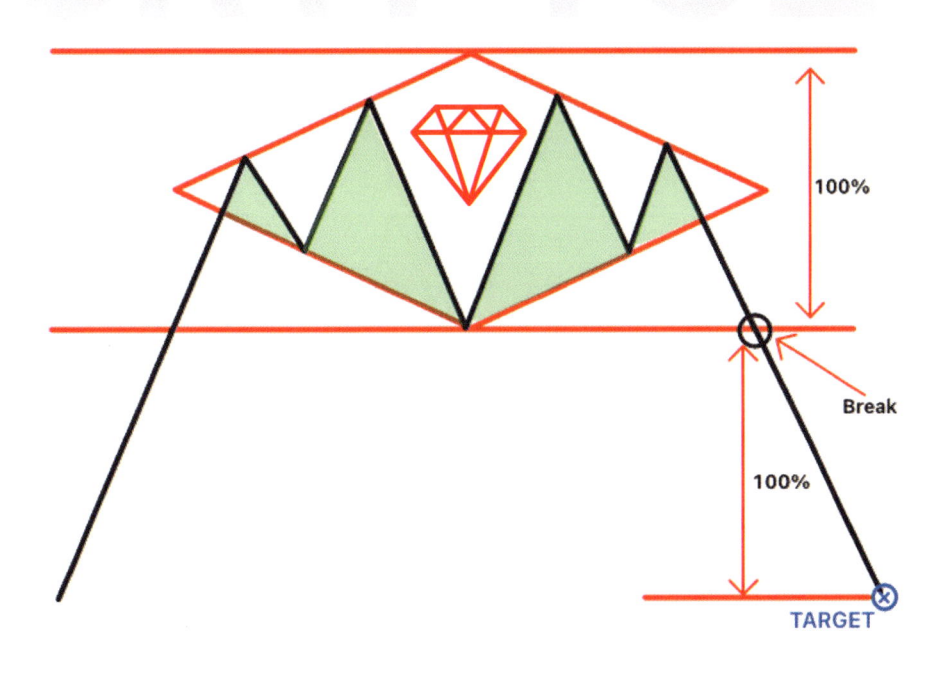

PATTERN "DIAMOND"

- The formation of the pattern occurs on higher timeframes (approximately 1 hour). A stronger indication of a reversal is presented with longer timeframes.
- The more evident and enduring a trend is in the market, the greater the impact of the pattern on the reversal.
- Additionally, if significant candles with minimal shadows break one side of the diamond during the pattern formation, it reinforces the pattern's strength.
- Confirming the likelihood of the pattern forming and playing out, pullbacks within the correction corridor aligning with previously tested crucial support/resistance levels is also significant.

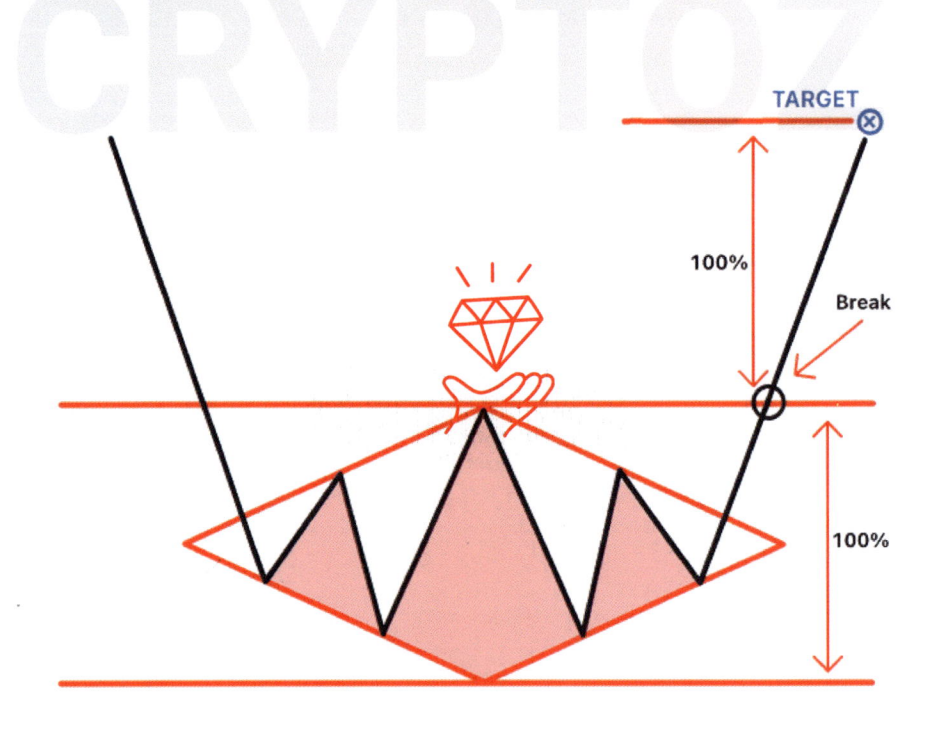

PARTERN "ADAM AND EVE"

A double bottom pattern known as Adam and Eve forms within a downtrend, with two distinct bottoms occurring before a price increase:

- The initial bottom resembles a V shape, known as Adam, with a peak on the support line.
- The second bottom takes the form of a U shape.

In this pattern:

- The first bottom (Adam) should exhibit a sharp price decline in a downtrend.
- The second bottom (Eve) follows the Adam shape, starting with a decline, a subsequent rise, and ultimately forming a U shape.

After the pattern breaks, consider opening a LONG position.
Set a target for closing the trade at a specific point.

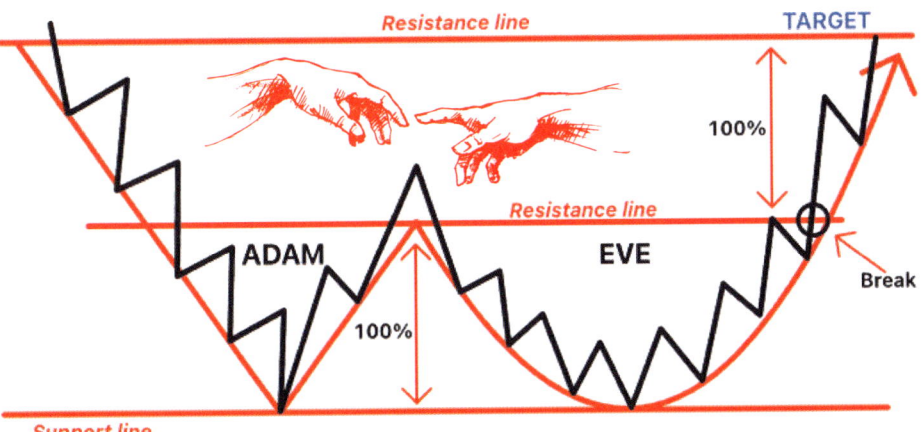

PATTERN "ADAM AND EVE"

A double bottom pattern known as Adam and Eve forms within a uptrande, with two distinct bottoms occurring before a price increase:

- The initial bottom resembles a V shape, known as Adam, with a peak on the support line.
- The second bottom takes the form of a U shape.

In this pattern:

- The first bottom (Adam) should exhibit a sharp price decline in a uptrend.
- The second bottom (Eve) follows the Adam shape, starting with a decline, a subsequent rise, and ultimately forming a U shape.

After the pattern breaks, consider opening a SHORT position. Set a target for closing the trade at a specific point.

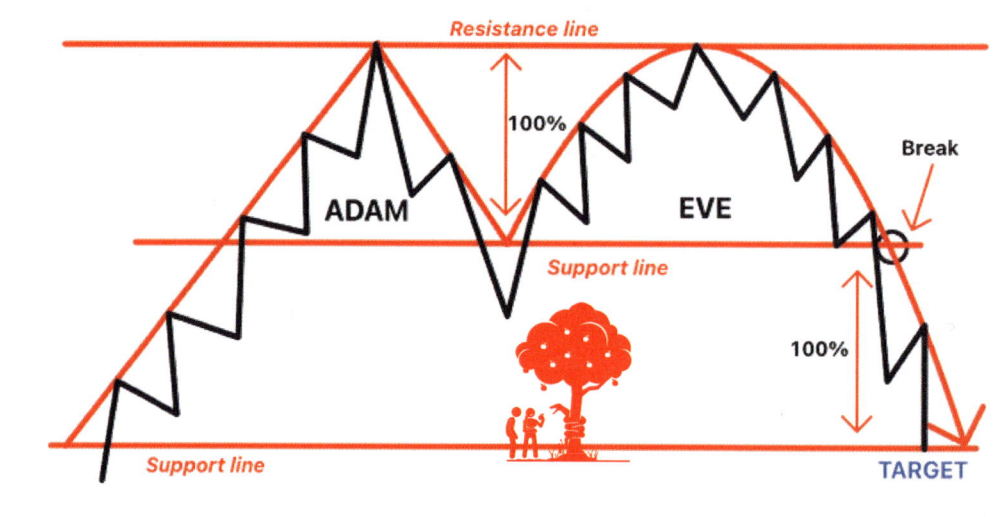

PATTERN "THREE VALEYS AND ARIVER"

Trading : Exploring the "Three Valleys and the River" Pattern
This pattern offers two trading opportunities.

- First trade: Look for a close above the trend line indicating a reversal. Open a "short" trade just above the breakout bar's high.

- Second trade: When 62% of the AB range is completed, initiate a "short" trade at point "C".

- Stop: For the first trade, if prices close below the trend line, close the trade. For the second trade, if prices close above level "C", close the trade.

- Target: Establish target levels for both trades. For the first trade (short setup of the three valleys), set the target between 62% and 78% of the AB range. For the second trade, aim for a 10% correction from point "C".

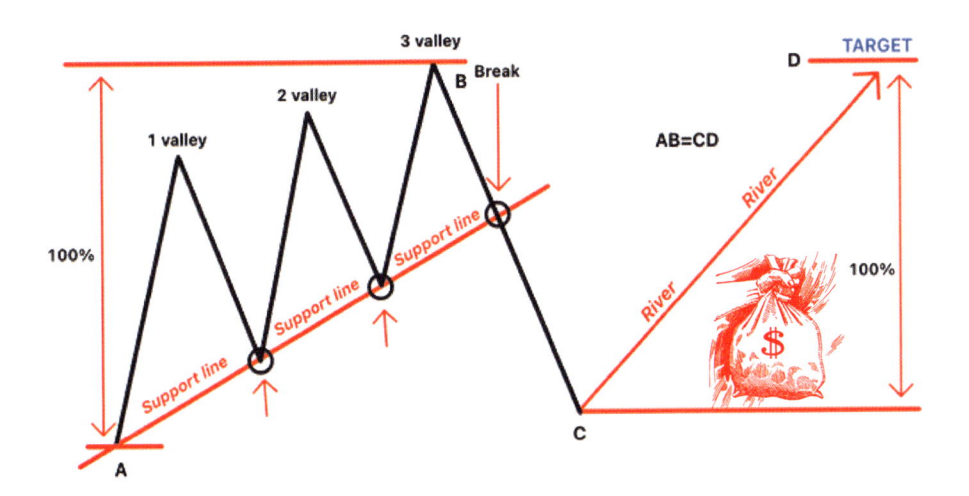

PATTERN "THREE VALLEYS AND A RIVER"

Trading : Exploring the "Three Valleys and the River" Pattern
This pattern offers two trading opportunities.

- First trade: Look for a close above the trend line indicating a reversal. Open a "long" trade just above the breakout bar's high.

- Second trade: When 62% of the AB range is completed, initiate a "long" trade at point "C".

- Stop: For the first trade, if prices close below the trend line, close the trade. For the second trade, if prices close above level "C", close the trade.

- Target: Establish target levels for both trades. For the first trade (long setup of the three valleys), set the target between 62% and 78% of the AB range. For the second trade, aim for a 10% correction from point "C".

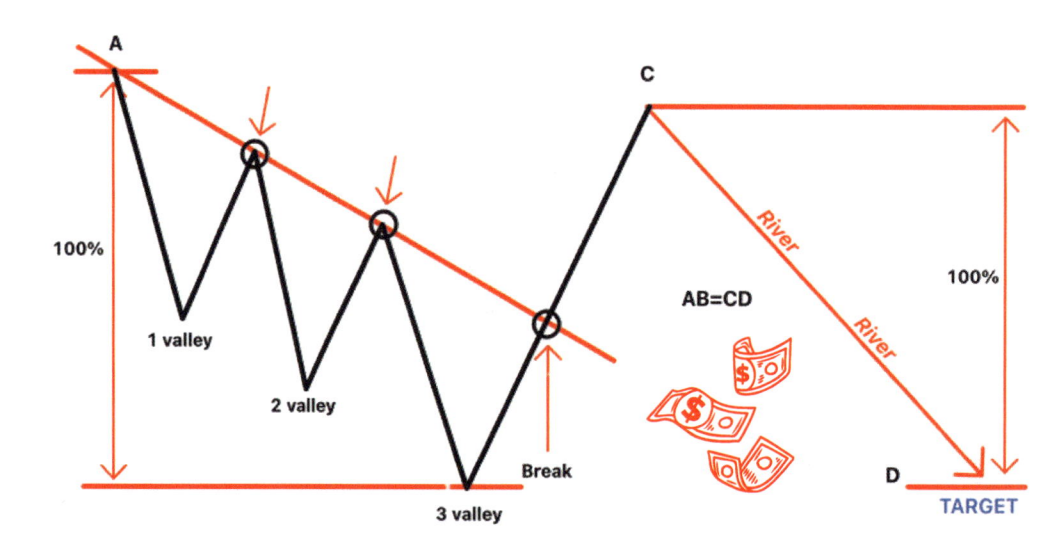

PATTERN "CAR'S EARS"

- Downtrend: Price shows a strong downward trend.

- Pause: Price halts for a while and moves sideways.

- "Left Ear": Price surges upwards, then quickly retreats, creating a pattern resembling a "left cat's ear".

- "Scalp": Price moves sideways again, forming a pattern resembling a "cat scalp".

- "Right Ear": Price surges upward once more, but retraces, forming a pattern resembling a "right cat's ear".

- Breakout: The downtrend persists as the price breaks through the "scalp line" (support line), continuing the downward trend.

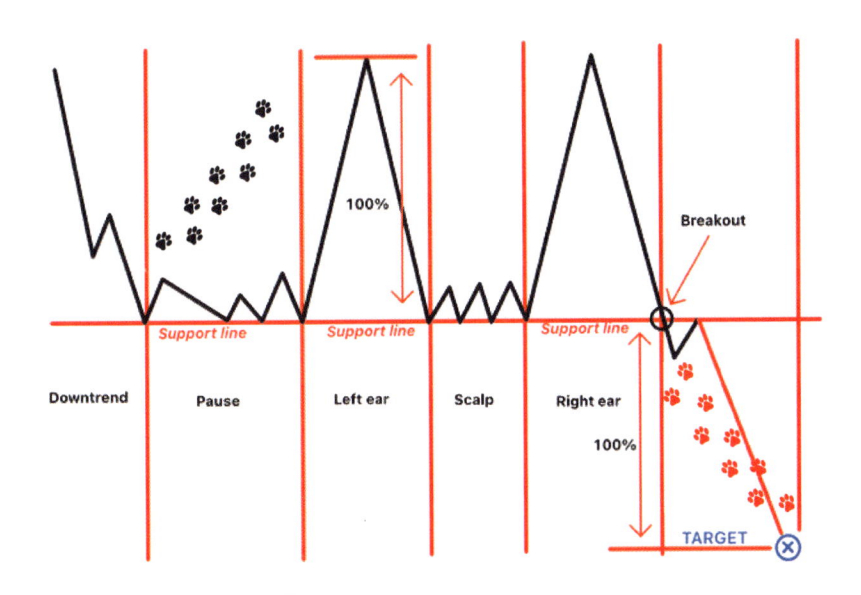

BUL PENNANT

The appearance of this pattern is typically preceded by a sharp price movement resembling an almost straight line, supported by a notable increase in trading volume.

Once an impulse reaches a particular significant price level, a small triangle-shaped "band" tends to emerge. This often indicates a continuation of the ongoing trend.

- TARGET (the designated point for closing an open trade)

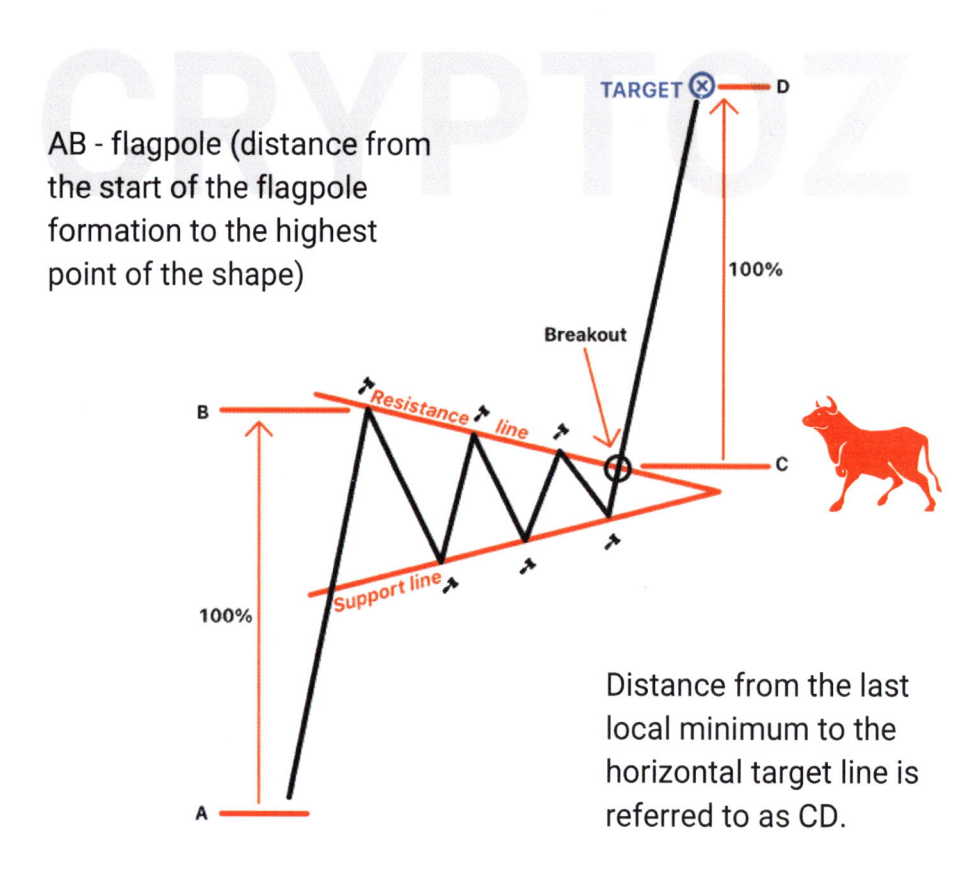

AB - flagpole (distance from the start of the flagpole formation to the highest point of the shape)

Distance from the last local minimum to the horizontal target line is referred to as CD.

BEAR PENNANT

The appearance of this pattern is typically foreshadowed by a sharp price movement resembling an almost straight line, paired with a substantial trading volume.

Once an impulse hits a particular significant price level, a small triangle-shaped "band" emerges. Subsequently, in most instances, the current trend progresses further.

TARGET - (the designated point to finalize an ongoing trade)

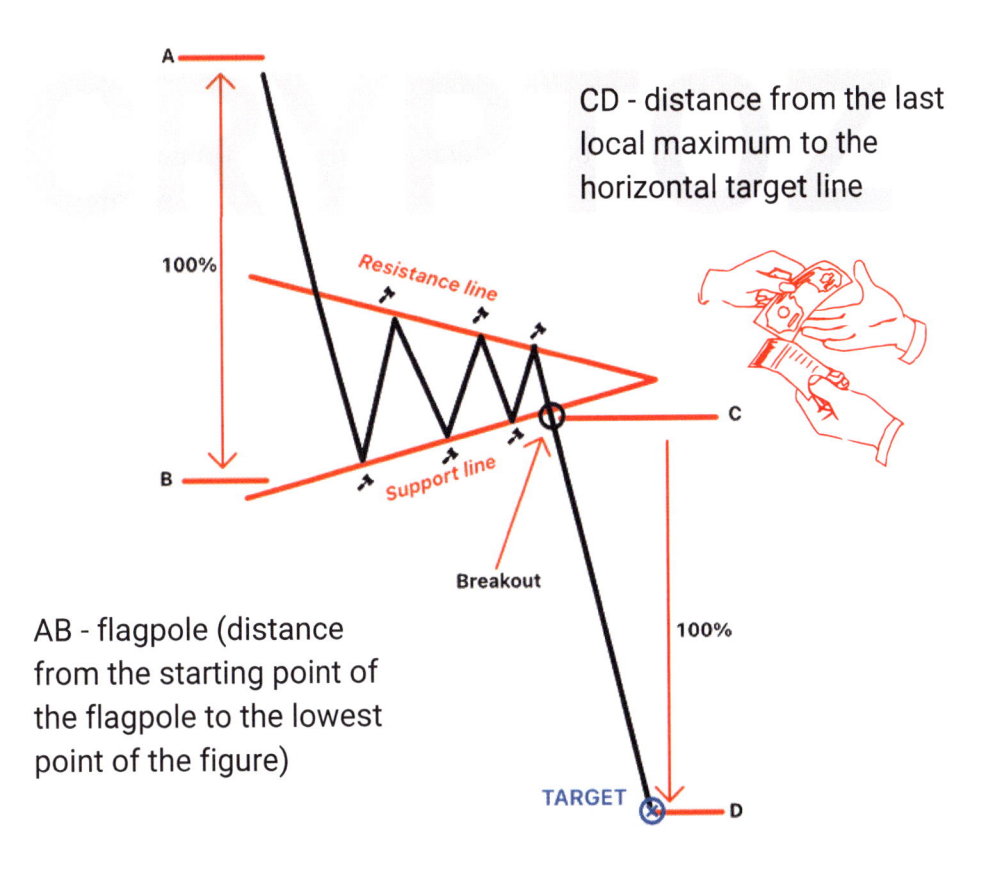

CD - distance from the last local maximum to the horizontal target line

AB - flagpole (distance from the starting point of the flagpole to the lowest point of the figure)

RISING WEDGE

- A rising wedge occurs when the price increase slows down, forming a narrowing pattern, with decreasing volume and volatility indicators.

- The highs and lows during the pattern formation are adjusted, resulting in minimal price fluctuations.

- Follow your trading strategy's algorithms rather than emotional impulses.

- It is advisable to enter a buy position after the pattern breaks.
- Set a target for closing your trade at your desired price level.

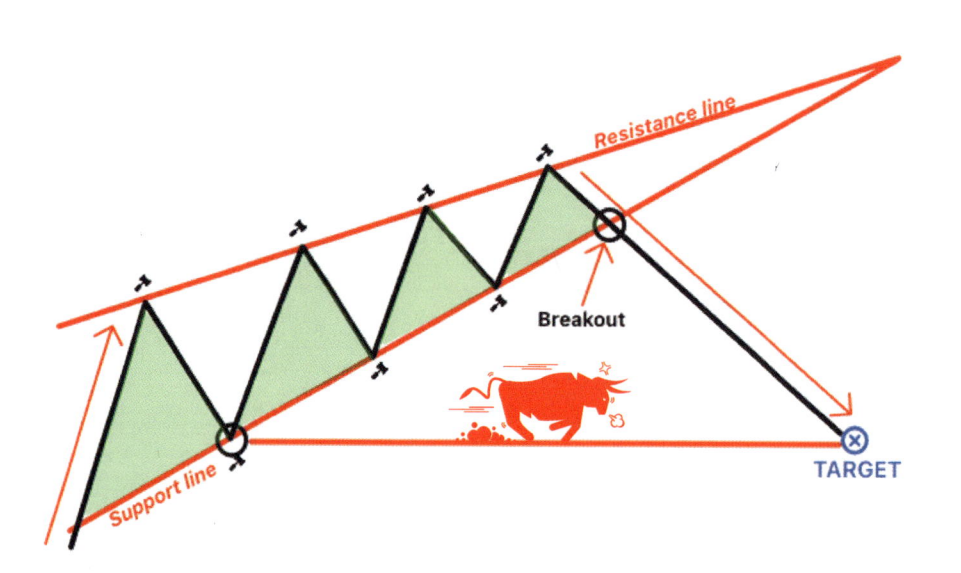

FALLING WEDGE

- A falling wedge occurs when the decline in prices slows down, creating a tapering pattern where volume and volatility indicators gradually decrease.
- The highs and lows are adjusted as the pattern forms, with prices falling or rising slightly.
- Stick to the algorithms of your trading strategy and avoid emotional decisions.
- Open a buying position once the pattern is broken.
- TARGET: the designated point to close the trade.

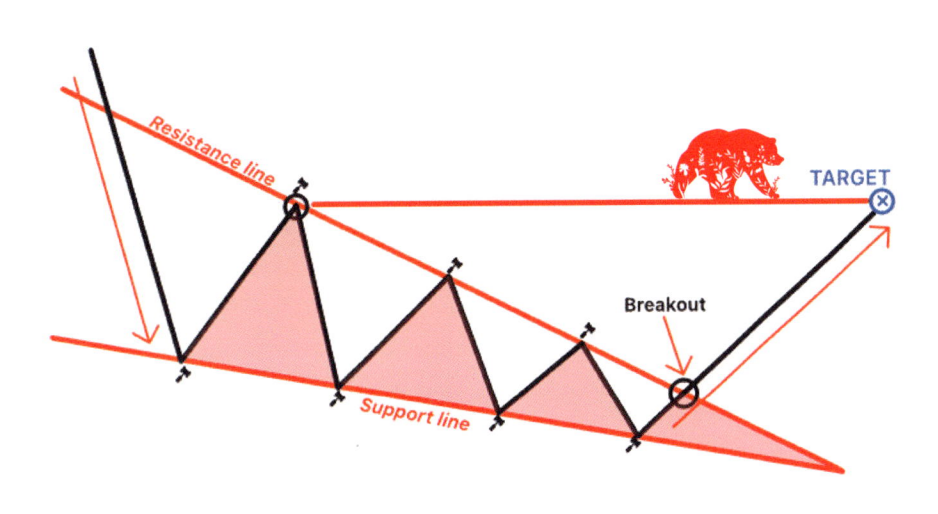

PATTERN "CUP AND HANDLE"

- A "Cup and handle" pattern begins to take shape with a bearish movement, which gradually slows down (curls) and transitions into a gradual bullish movement, creating a distinctive shape on the chart.

- Following the formation of the "Cup," the next essential component of the pattern emerges, known as the "Handle." After reaching the peak on the right side of the "Cup," a slight pullback occurs, forming the "Handle" to its right.

- Typically, at the peak of the "Cup," the volumes are at their lowest. Subsequently, as the second part of the "Cup" develops, the volumes should gradually increase.

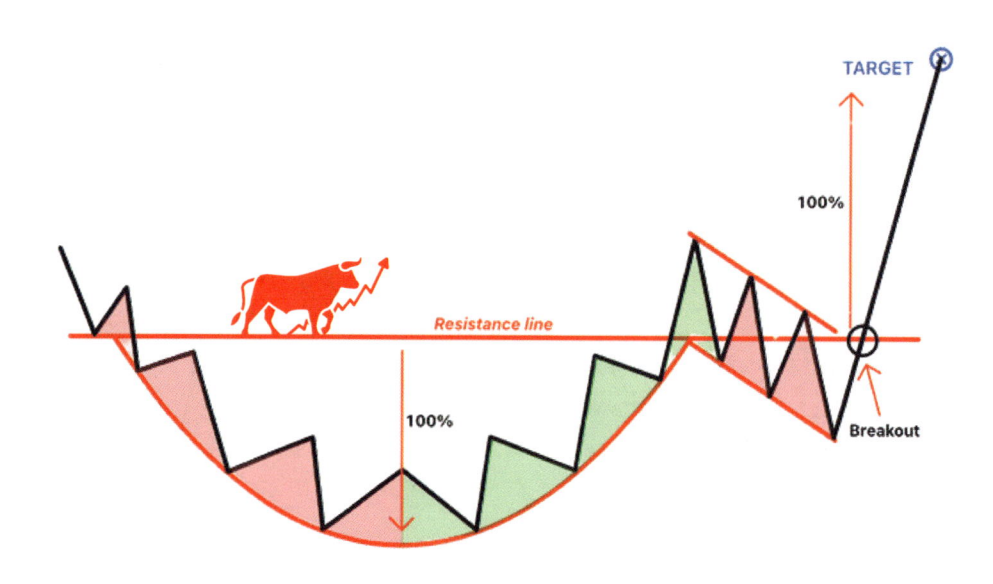

PARTERN " BEARISH CUP AND HANDLE"

- The "Bear-cup and handle" pattern initiates with a bullish movement that gradually slows down, bends, and transitions into a slow bearish movement, shaping a pattern on the chart.

- Following the formation of the "Cup," the second essential element of the pattern emerges, known as the "Handle." Once the low point on the right side of the "Cup" is formed, a minor pullback occurs to the right, creating the "Handle."

- Typically, the "Inverted Cup" pattern reaches its lowest point at the top. Subsequently, the volume levels should progressively increase during the development of the second part of the "Inverted Cup."

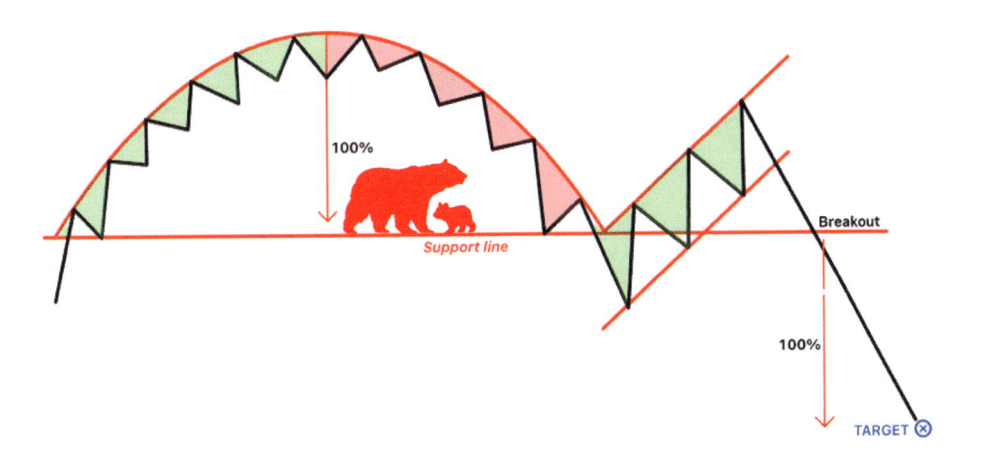

BULLISH FLAG

- A distinct pattern typically appears following a sharp price movement resembling an almost straight line, coupled with a notable trading volume.
- During the formation stage, volume indicators tend to decrease gradually.
- Frequently, "Flags" start to take shape around the midpoint of the price movement.
- Consequently, after the breakout occurs, the price is expected to cover the same distance as before the formation of this pattern.

- TARGET: The designated point to close an open trade.

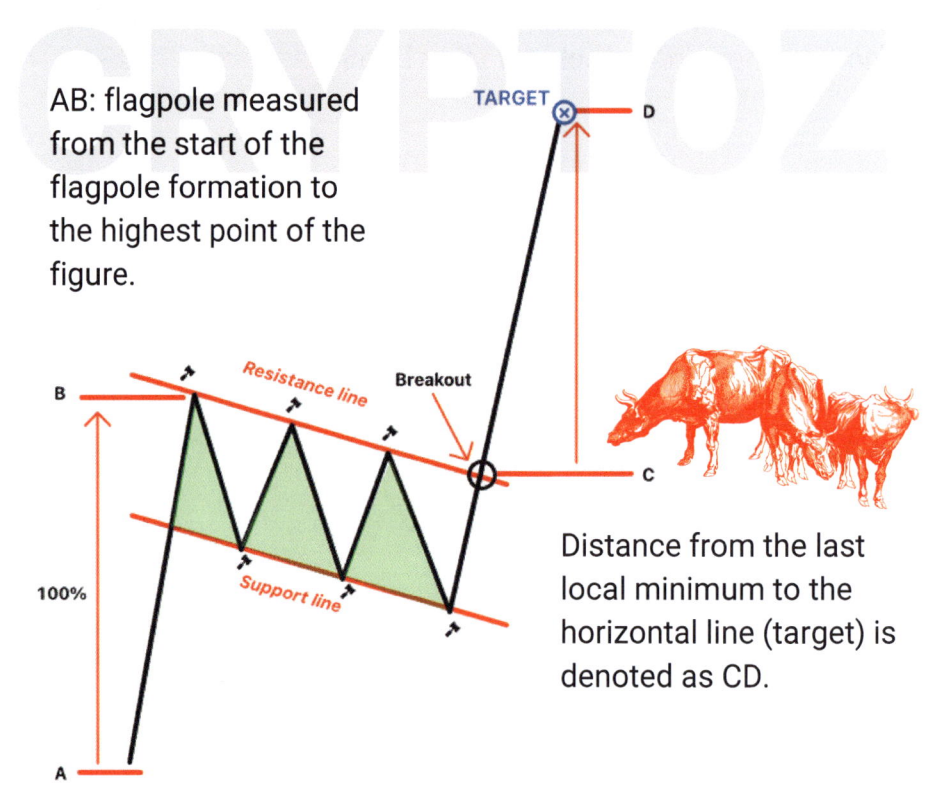

AB: flagpole measured from the start of the flagpole formation to the highest point of the figure.

Distance from the last local minimum to the horizontal line (target) is denoted as CD.

BEARISH FLAG

- Before such a pattern appears, there is a notable price surge resembling an almost straight line, coupled with substantial trading volume.

- During the formation phase, volume indicators tend to decrease gradually.
- Frequently, "Flags" materialize around the midpoint of the price movement. Subsequently, after the breakout, the price should cover the same distance as before the formation of this pattern.

- TARGET - (the point to consider closing an open trade)

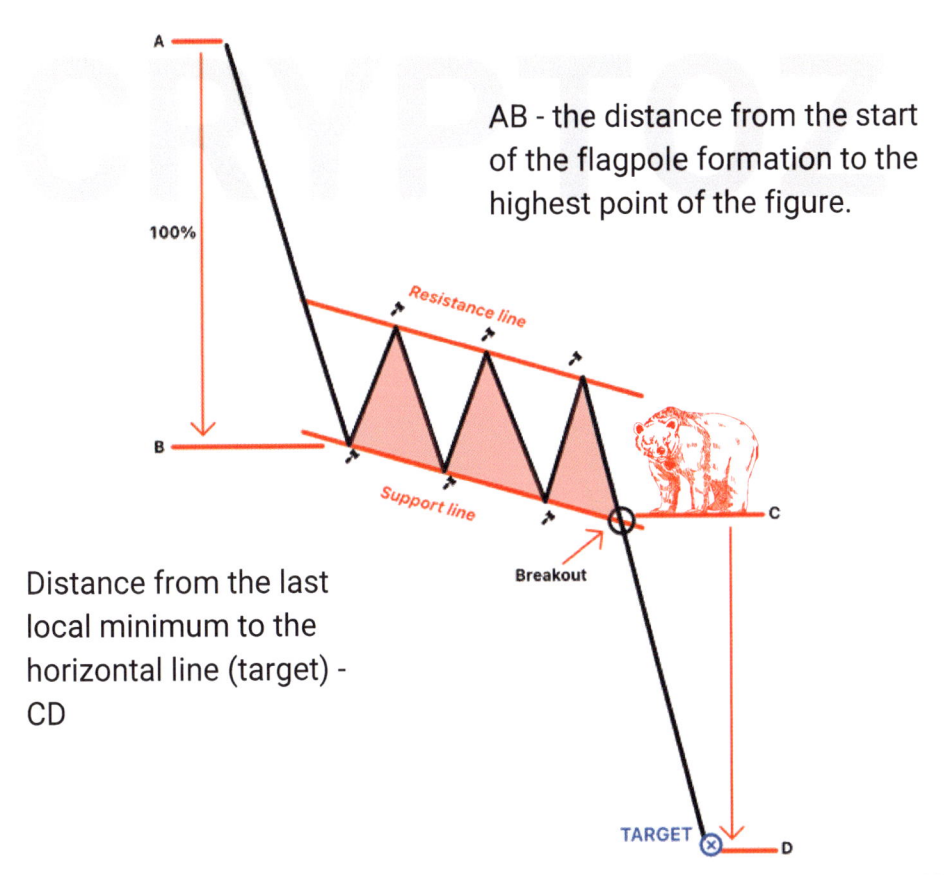

AB - the distance from the start of the flagpole formation to the highest point of the figure.

Distance from the last local minimum to the horizontal line (target) - CD

BULLISH RECTANGLE

- In a bullish trend, when a pattern emerges and the price rises upwards, it is identified as a bullish rectangle.

- A rectangle shape requires a minimum of four touch points to take form.

- Typically, the price breakthrough aligns with the prior trend direction, establishing the rectangle as a trend continuation.

- The rectangle pattern is confirmed only after the price surpasses the resistance line.

- Entry points can be selected either after the pattern break or following a re-test, if applicable.

- TARGET: the designated point for closing an open trade.

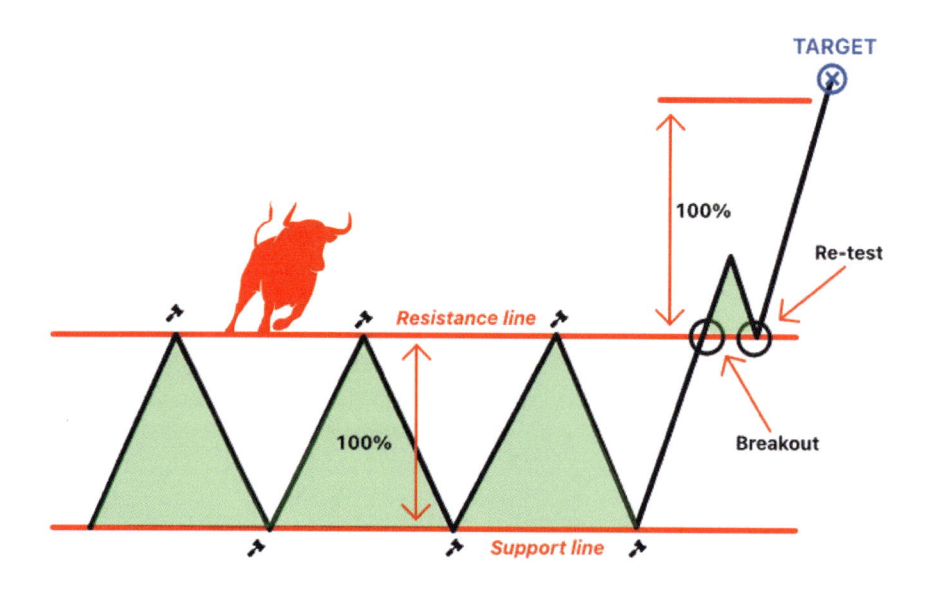

BEARISH RECTANGLE

- If this pattern emerges during a bearish trend and the price breaks downwards, it is termed a bearish rectangle.

- At least four touch points are required to outline a rectangle shape.

- Typically, the price breakthrough aligns with the preceding trend's direction, labeling the rectangle as a continuation of the trend.

- The formation of the rectangle pattern is confirmed once the price breaches the support line.

- An entry can be executed post the figure's breakout or upon any subsequent re-test.

- TARGET - (the designated point to conclude an ongoing trade)

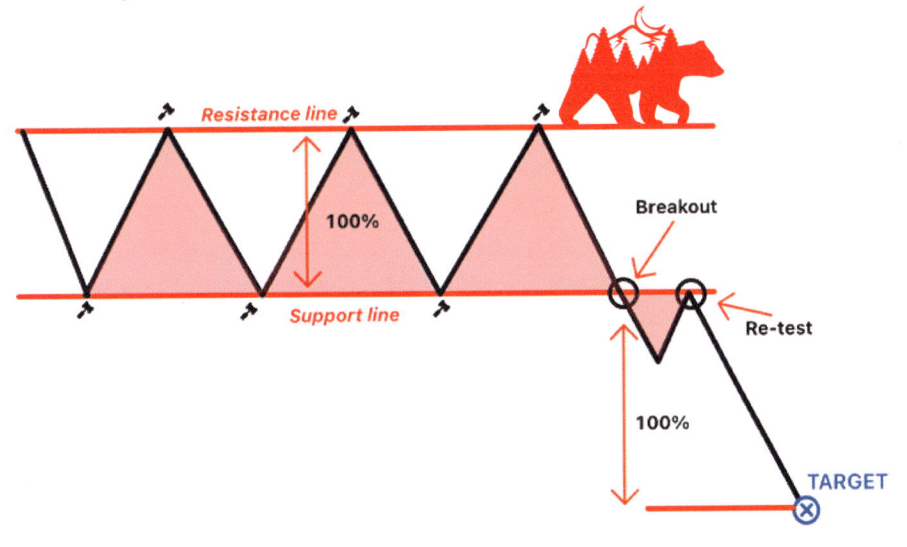

BULLISH 5-0 PATTERN

When entering a bullish or bearish formation at point D, validate the support/resistance level to determine whether to go long or short:

- Once in the trade, place the Stop-Loss beyond the boundaries of the rising/descending trend channel from the entry point, based on the bullish or bearish pattern. For a bullish pattern, position it below the support, and for a bearish pattern when going short, position it behind the channel resistance (downtrend).
- Point O marks the beginning of the downward movement, point M indicates the first upward correction, point A signifies the end of the correction and the start of the downward movement, while point B denotes the end of the downfall and the start of the upward movement, positioned between 1.13-1.618 from XA. Point C signals the end of a strong upward movement, ideally positioned between 1.618-2.24 from AB. Point D marks the end of the downfall and the start of the upward movement, which is the entry point in this scenario. Entry should be placed at the 50% correction level from BC.

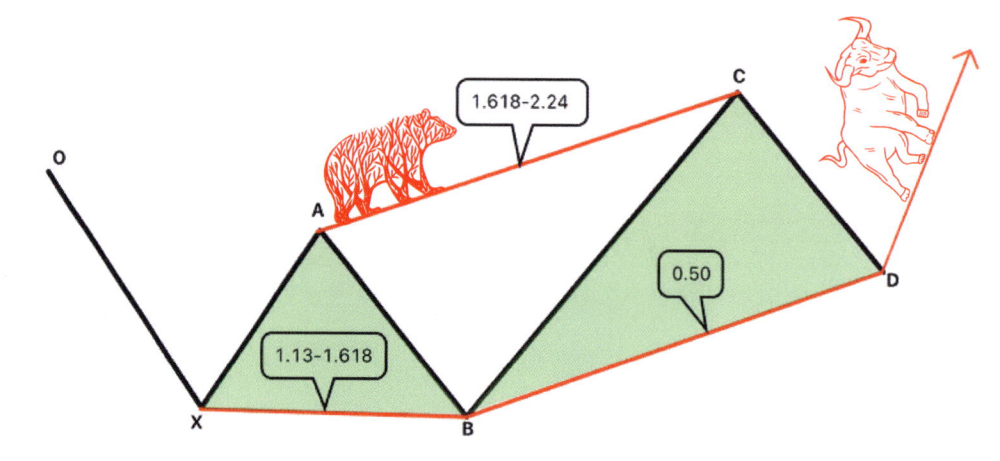

BEARISH 5-0 PATTERN

- To enter a bullish or bearish formation at point D, confirm the support/resistance level to decide whether to go long or short.

- Once the trade is initiated, place the Stop-Loss behind the boundaries of the ascending/descending trend channel from the entry point, based on the bullish or bearish pattern. For a bullish pattern, position it below support, and for a bearish pattern when going short, position it behind channel resistance (downtrend).

- Point O marks the beginning of growth and pattern formation, point X indicates the start of a downward correction, point A signifies the beginning of growth and the end of correction, point B marks the end of price growth, ideally falling within the Fibonacci projection range between 1.13-1.618. Point C denotes the conclusion of a significant decline and the start of growth, while point D signifies the end of growth, marking the ideal position to initiate a sell transaction, ideally at the 50% correction level from IS.

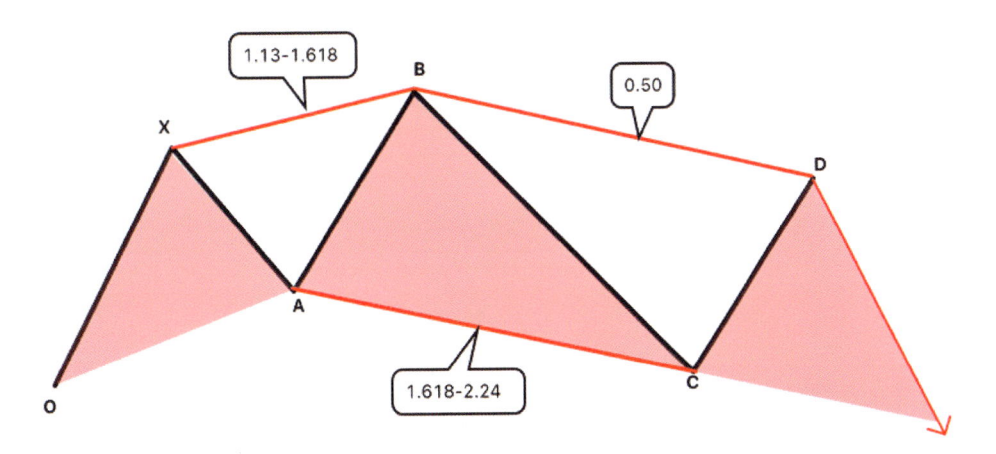

PATRERN "MEASURED MOVE UP"

"Measuring Move" Breakdown into 3 Stages (Related Trends):

- The First Stage (Trend):
    - The trend initiates from the extreme point of the previous trend and progresses over a period ranging from several weeks to several months. During this phase, a distinct directional price range is established.
- The Second Stage (Trend):
    - This phase acts as a corrective measure and is the shortest among the three stages. Typically, its duration is around half of the first stage's timeframe. Normally, prices correct by 30-70% based on the length of the initial decline. In cases where the first phase extends over a significant period, such as a year, the corrective movement will be more extensive and prolonged. While there may be multiple smaller-scale patterns, focus on the overall trend movement and the corrective action in the middle of the pattern. Occasionally, there are reversal patterns before this stage, like double bottoms, triple bottoms, inverted head and shoulders, among others.
- The Third Stage (Trend):
    - The third trend mirrors the first in terms of duration and dynamics. Targets are determined during this phase, based on the percentage of the initial decline before the corrective movement of the second phase.

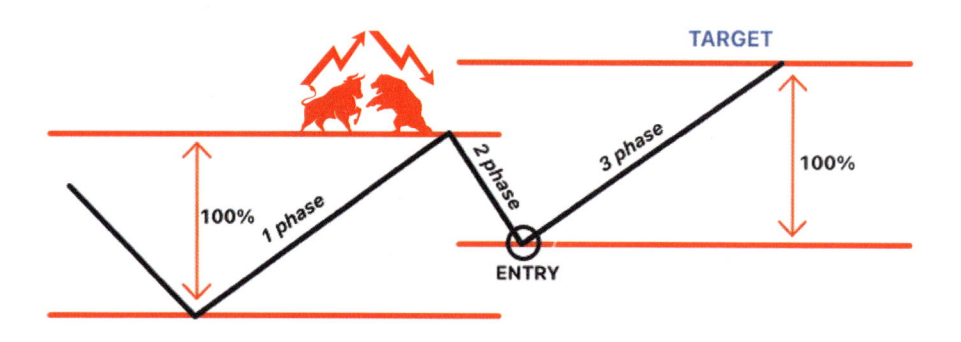

PATTERN "MEASURED MOVE DOWN"

"Measuring Move" encompasses three stages (related trends):

- The initial stage (trend):
  - This trend begins from the extreme point of the previous trend and evolves over a period ranging from several weeks to several months. During this stage, a distinct directional price corridor is established.
- The second stage (trend):
  - Acting as a corrective phase, this is the shortest of the three stages, typically lasting about half the duration of the first stage. The price is usually corrected by 30-70%, depending on the length of the initial decline. If the first phase lasts an extended period, such as a year, the corrective movement will be more substantial and prolonged. While there may be numerous smaller-scale patterns, the overall trend movement and the corrective action in the middle of the pattern should be observed. Sometimes, there are reversal patterns before the second phase, like double or triple bottoms, inverted head and shoulders, among others.
- The third stage (trend):
  - The final trend is approximately equal in duration and dynamics to the first one. Goals are calculated in this phase based on the percentages of the initial drop to the corrective movement of the second stage.

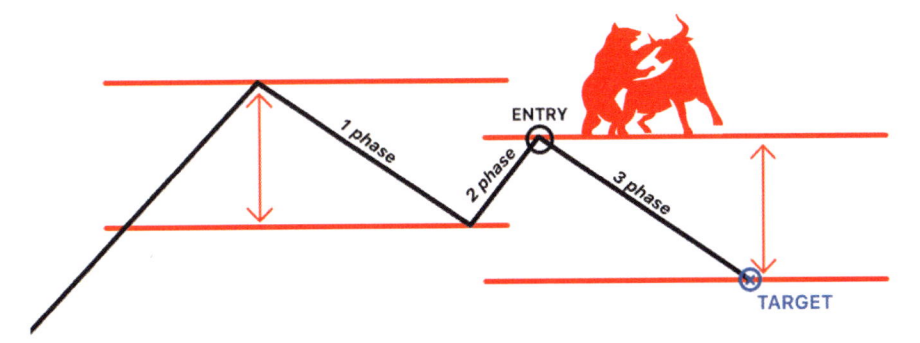

ASCENDING TRIANGLE

- The upper edge acts as a horizontal resistance line, while the lower edge functions as an oblique support line.

- The price surpasses the horizontal resistance line.

- To forecast the price movement target, measure the widest part of the pattern and place it at the triangle breakout point.

- In the formation of an upward triangle, there is a decrease in volume indicators.

- The ultimate confirmation of an ascending triangle is the breach of the upper resistance line, which then transforms into the lower support line.

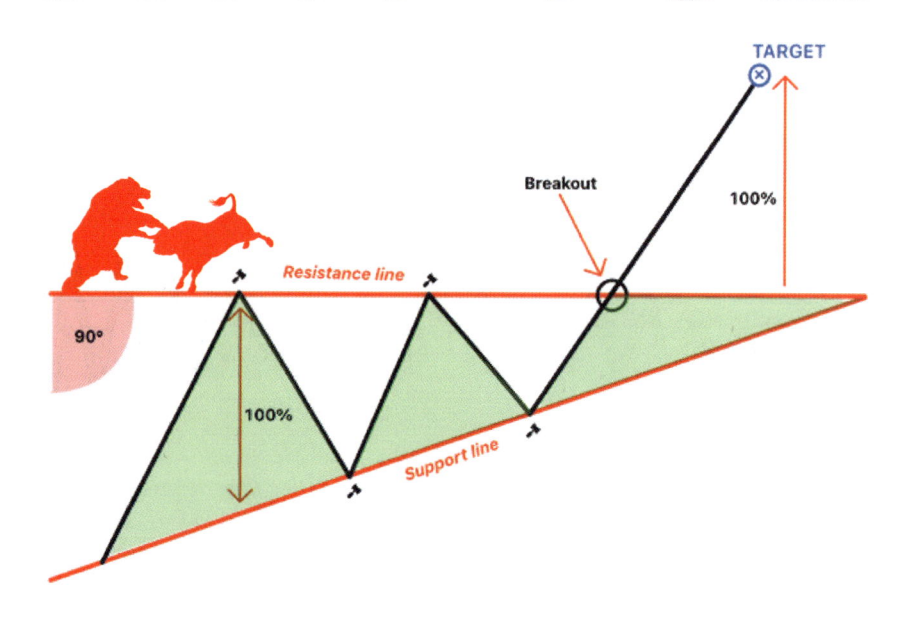

DESCENDING TRIANGLE

- The upper edge acts as a slanted resistance line, while the lower edge serves as a horizontal support line.

- The price breaches the horizontal support line.

- To predict the price target movement, measure the widest part of the pattern and project it from the triangle breakout point.

- Decreased volume indicators are observed during the formation of the descending triangle.

- The definitive signal of a descending triangle is the breach of the lower support line, now transitioning to become the upper resistance line.

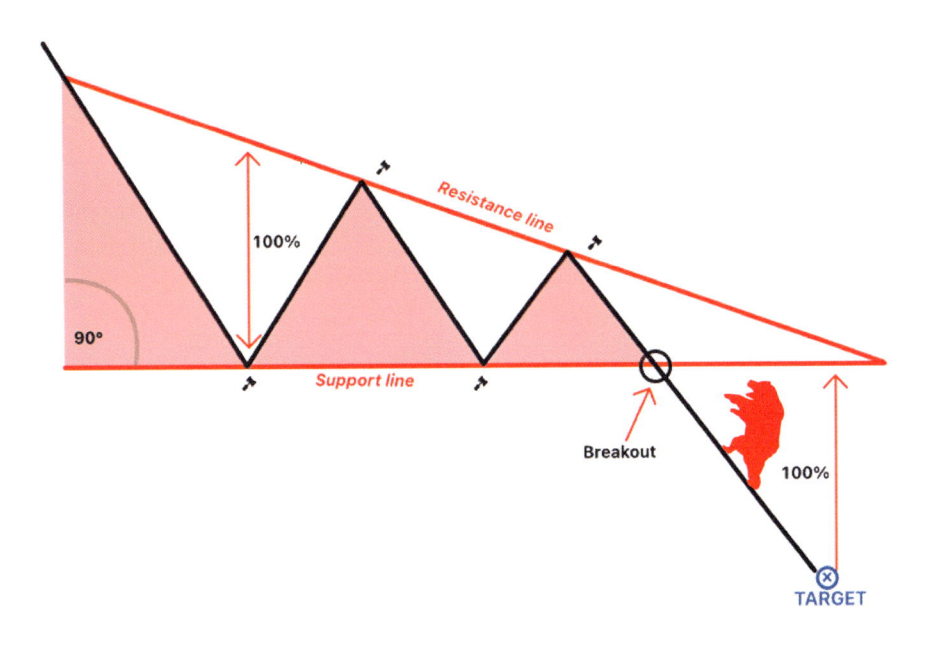

PARTERN "BULLISH CRAB"

This model resembles a butterfly, with slightly adjusted parameters. Introduced by Scott Carney in 2000, the crab pattern is known for its accuracy in identifying potential reversal zones, which proves effective in the majority of cases.

- The second phase of this pattern can be either an ascending wedge or a descending wedge, depending on whether it's a bearish or bullish crab formation. This aspect works effectively in traditional trading methods without the need for additional harmony.

This feature contributes to the profitability of this formation.

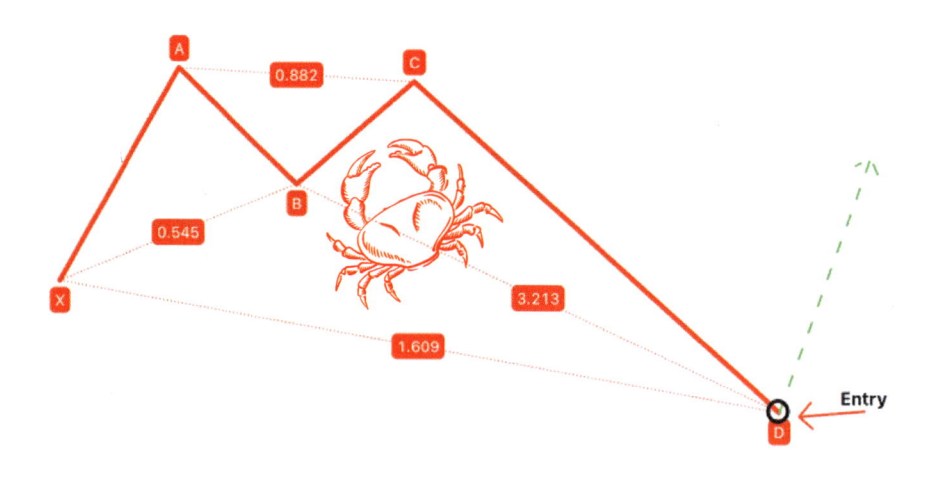

PATTERN "BEARISH CRAB"

This model resembles a butterfly pattern, but with slightly different parameters. Scott Carney introduced this pattern in 2000. The crab is considered one of the most precise harmonic patterns due to its potential reversal zone, which proves effective in the majority of cases.

- The second segment of the pattern can be either an ascending wedge or a descending wedge, based on whether it is a bearish or bullish crab formation. This aspect functions effectively in traditional trading without any harmonic elements.

This formation offers good profitability.

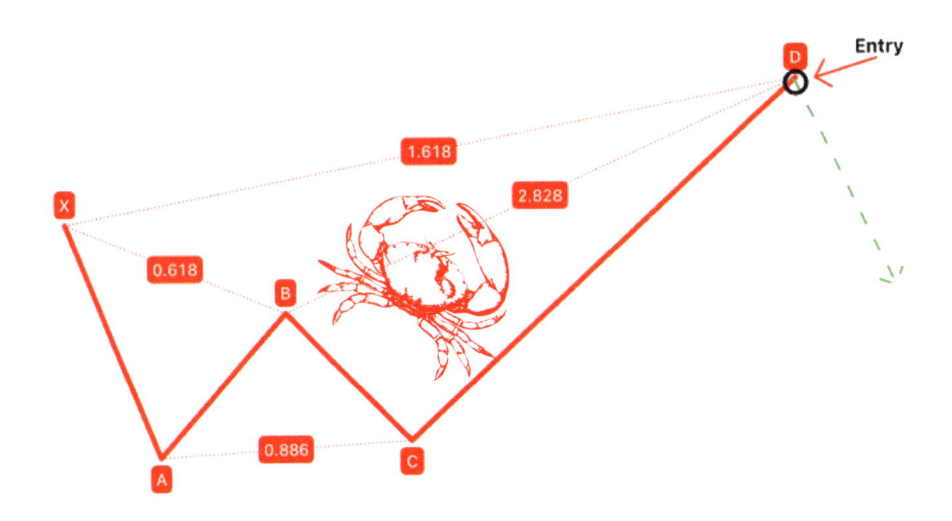

PATTERN "BULISH BATRERFLY"

- One of the most popular harmonic patterns is the Gartley pattern, known for its high degree of precision. This corrective pattern signifies the continuation of the current trend.
    - The primary trend briefly alters its course before reverting to its original direction, displaying a temporary correction in the ABCD pattern form.
- A bullish pattern typically emerges early in a trend, denoting the conclusion of corrective waves. The region at point D is identified as the potential reversal zone. To ensure an upward movement, consider entering at point D or slightly above it. Place a stop loss near the entry point.

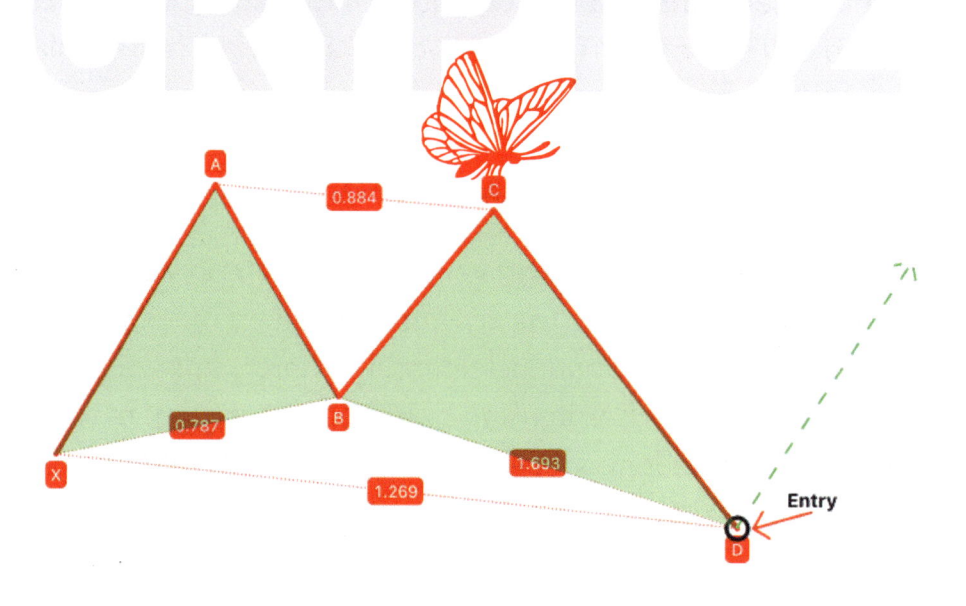

PARTERN "BEARISH BATTERFLY"

- One of the most popular harmonic patterns is the Gartley pattern, known for its high level of precision. This pattern serves as a corrective signal, indicating the continuation of the current trend. In this scenario, the primary trend briefly shifts before reverting to its original path, showcasing a temporary ABCD correction shape.

- A bearish pattern typically emerges early in a trend and signifies the conclusion of corrective waves. The region around point D is referred to as a potential reversal zone. Consider entering at point D or slightly above it to ensure a more secure downward movement. Place a stop loss near the entry point for added protection.

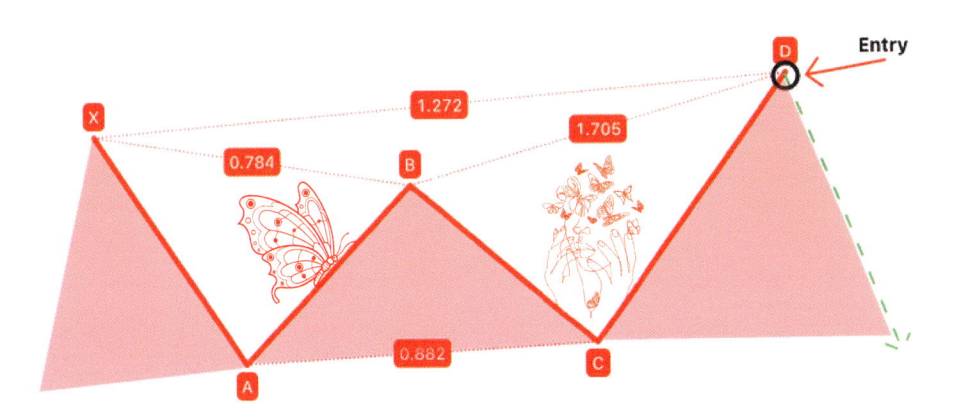

PATTERN "BEARISH BAT"

- In the case of a bearish "Bat" formation, it is advisable to initiate a sell trade around point D. The bearish pattern "Bar" in traditional trading signifies a continuation of a trend following the completion of the pattern – like a double bottom or a part of the "Dragon" formation.

- Interestingly, both models are personal favorites due to their effectiveness and minimal false signals. Therefore, when identified and entered correctly, the "Bar" pattern offers reliable signals and few false alarms.

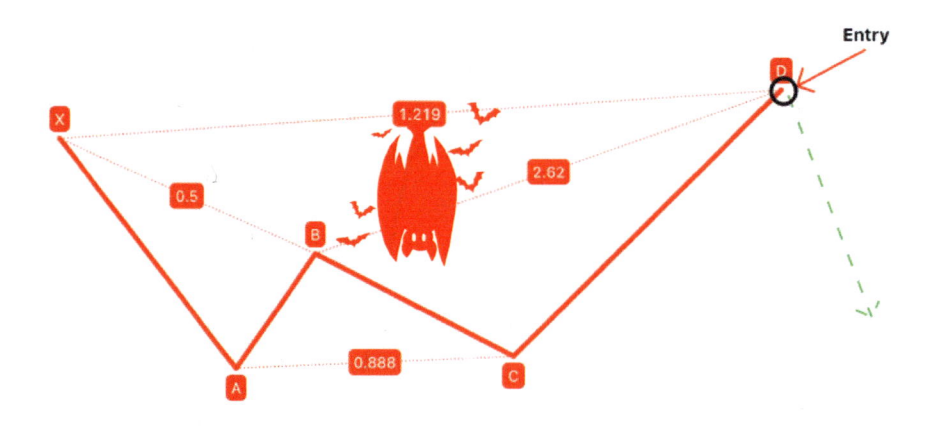

PATTERN "BULLISH BAT"

- When a bullish "Bat" formation occurs, consider initiating a sell trade around point D. The classical trading pattern "Bat" signifies a continuation of the trend after the completion of the pattern, such as a double top, or as part of the formation of a "Dragon". Interestingly, these two models are my top picks for accuracy and provide minimal false signals. Consequently, correctly identifying and entering the "Bat" pattern results in reliable signals and few false alarms.

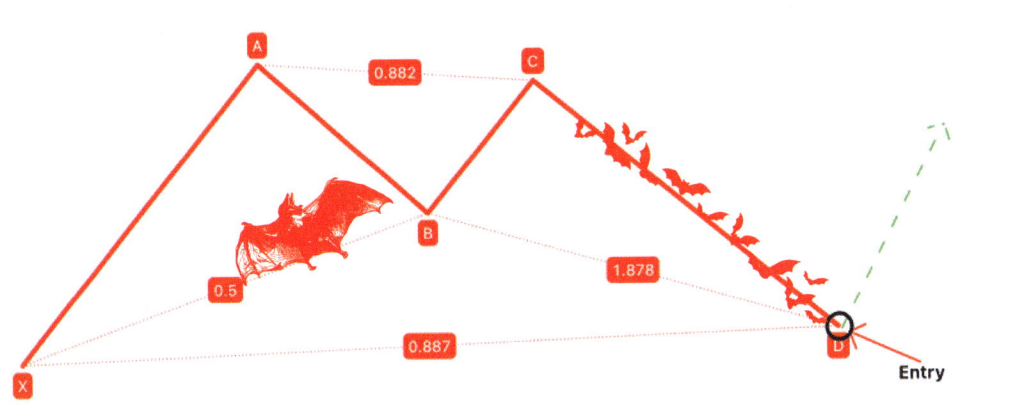

TREND REVERSAL PATTERNS

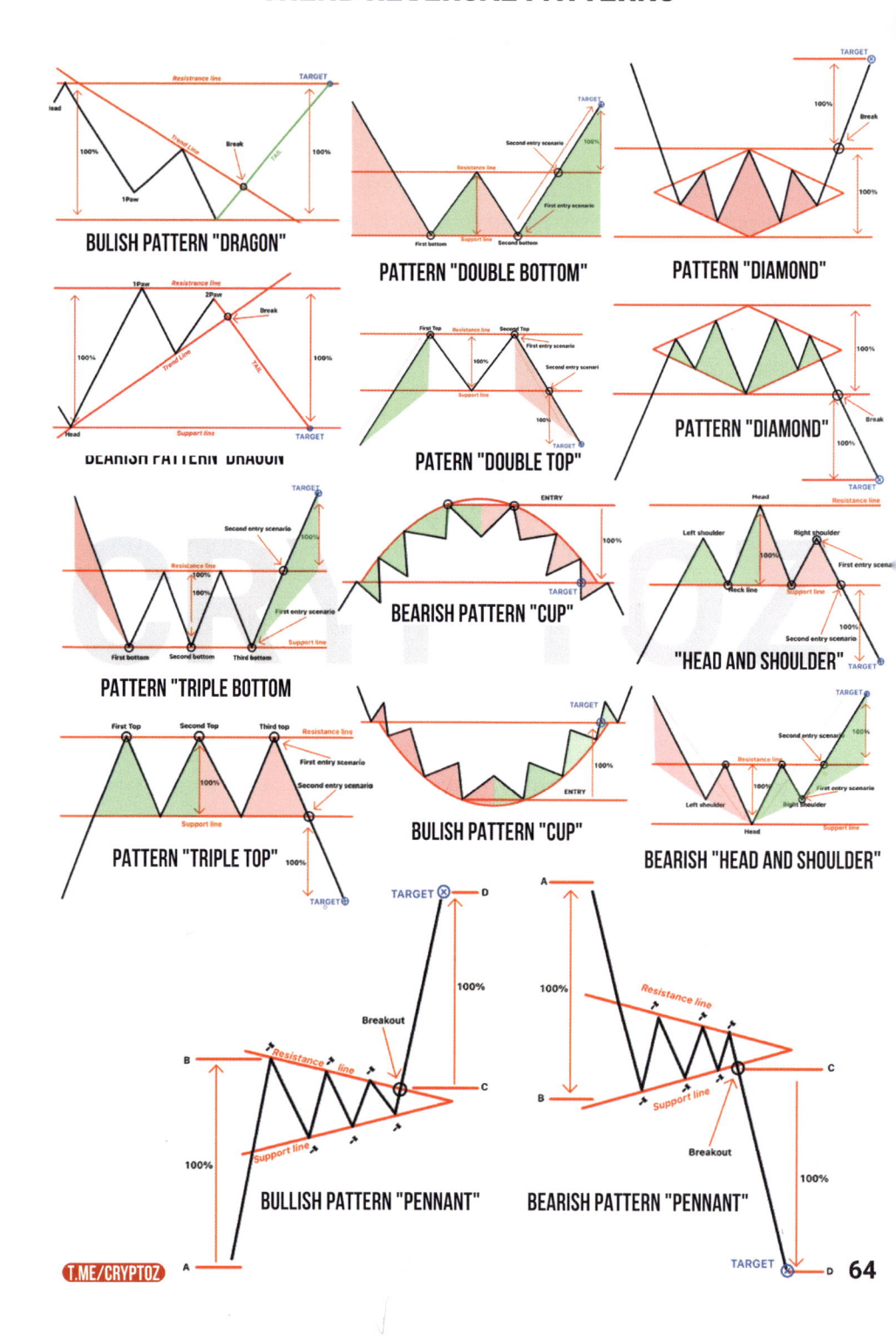

CONTINUATION PATTERNS

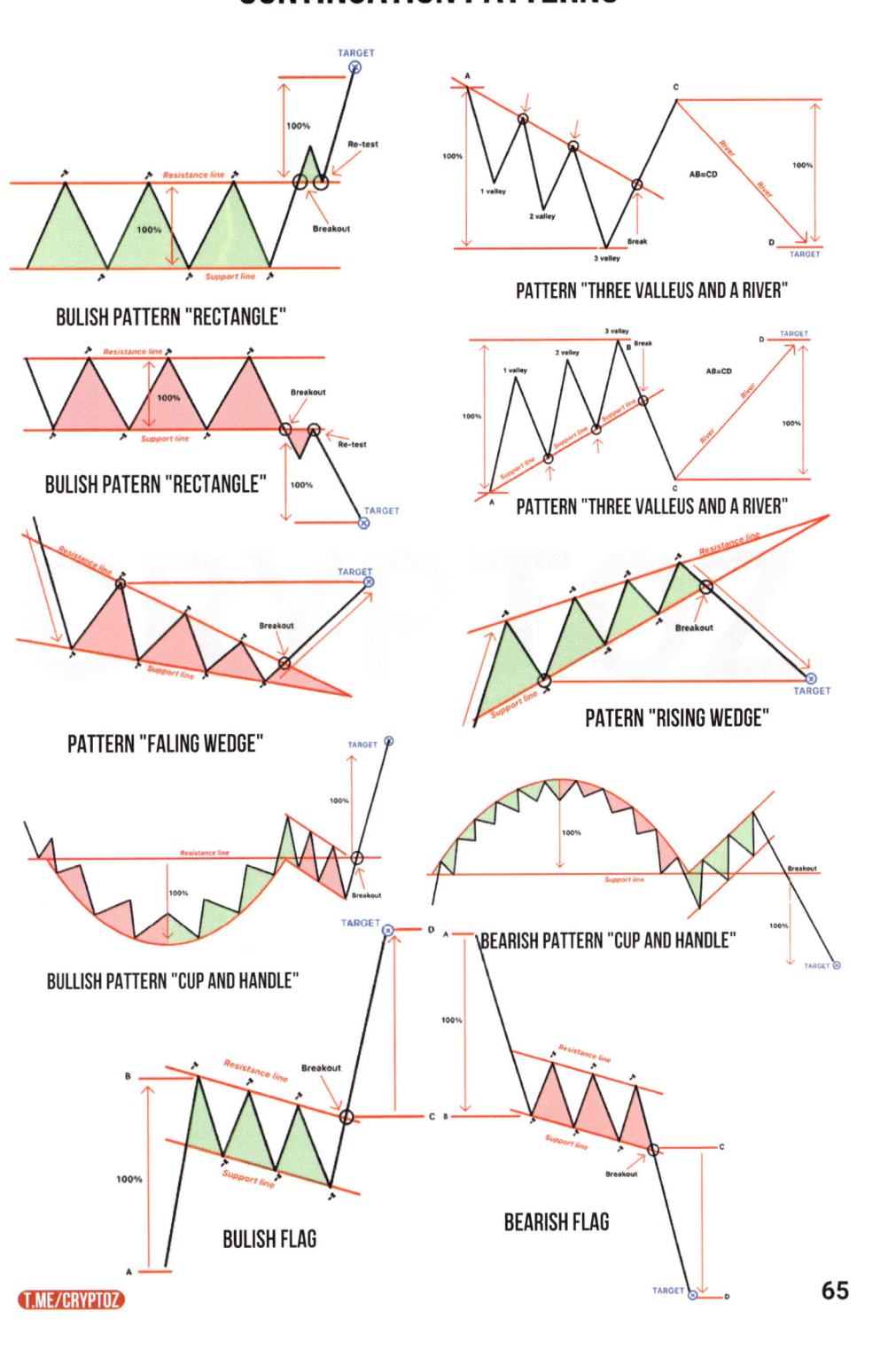

BULISH PATTERN "RECTANGLE"

BULISH PATERN "RECTANGLE"

PATTERN "FALING WEDGE"

BULLISH PATTERN "CUP AND HANDLE"

BULISH FLAG

PATTERN "THREE VALLEUS AND A RIVER"

PATTERN "THREE VALLEUS AND A RIVER"

PATERN "RISING WEDGE"

BEARISH PATTERN "CUP AND HANDLE"

BEARISH FLAG

TREND REVERSAL PATTERNS

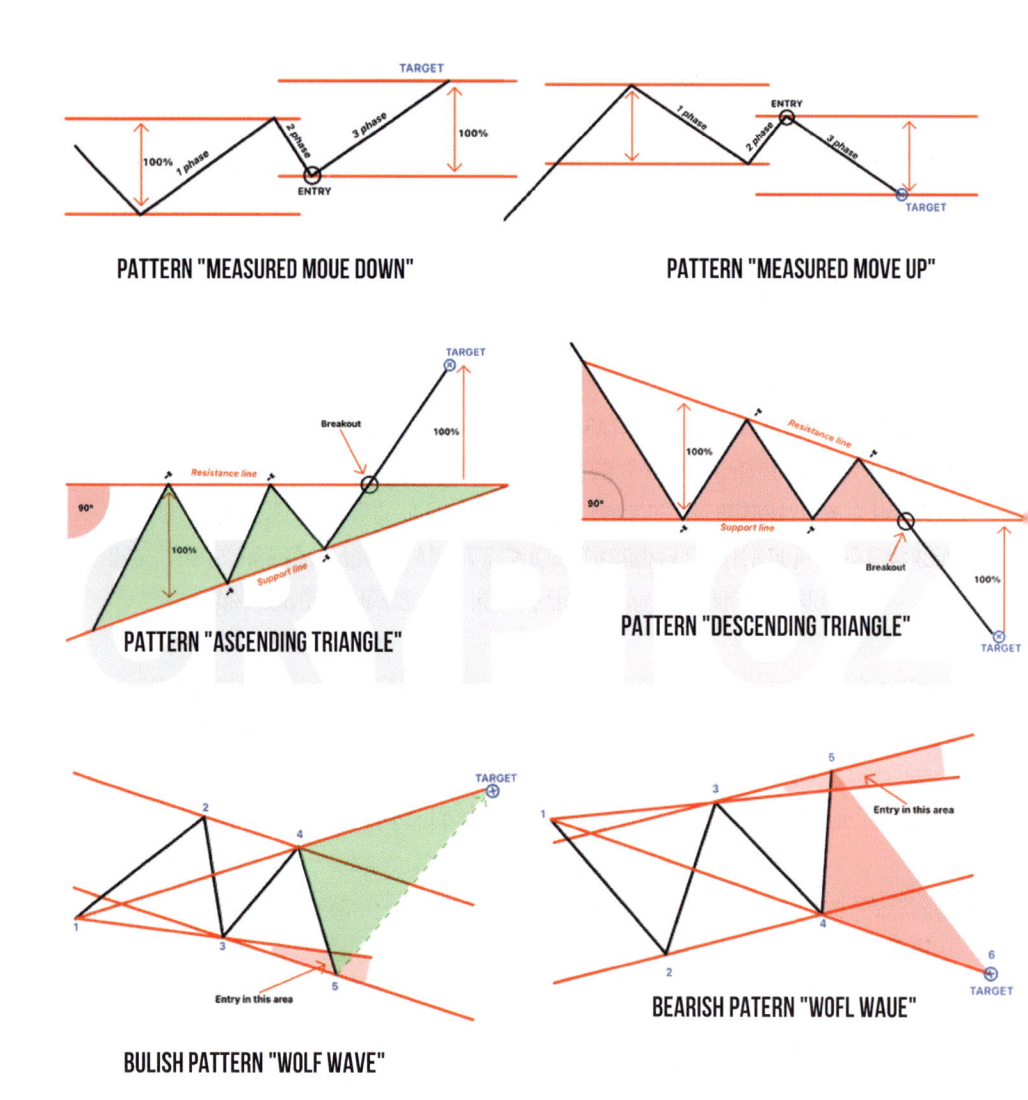

PATTERN "MEASURED MOVE DOWN"

PATTERN "MEASURED MOVE UP"

PATTERN "ASCENDING TRIANGLE"

PATTERN "DESCENDING TRIANGLE"

BULISH PATTERN "WOLF WAVE"

BEARISH PATERN "WOFL WAUE"

HARMONIC PATTERNS

BULISH PATTERN "BUTERFLY"

BEARISH PATTERN "BUTERFLY"

BULISH PATTERN "BAT"

BEARISH PARTERN "BAT"

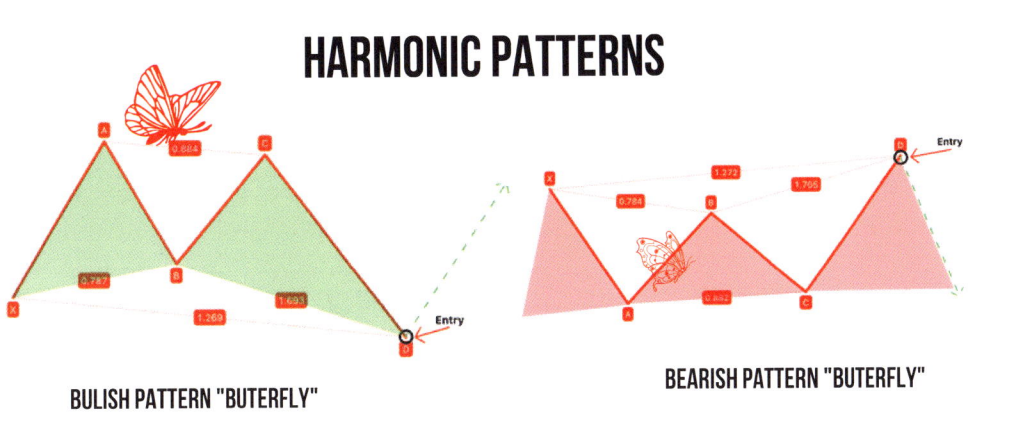

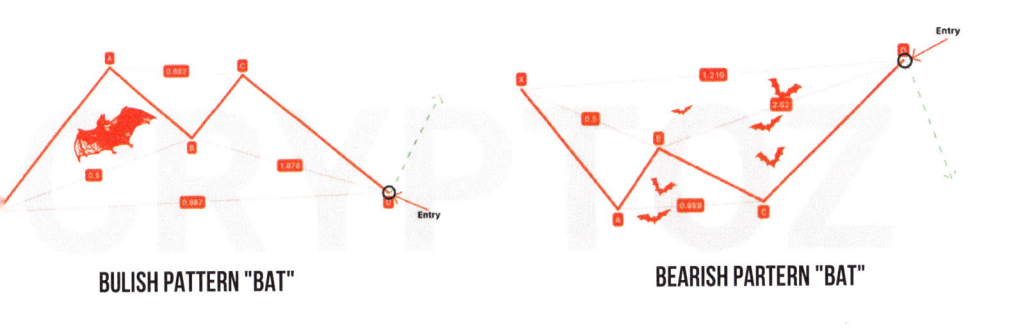

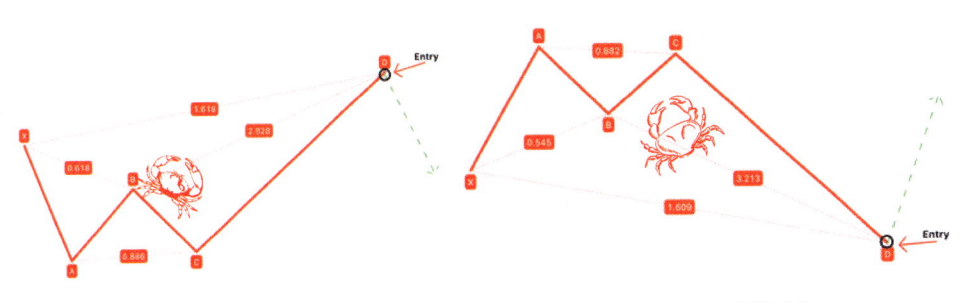

BULISH PATTERN "CRAB"

BEARISH PARFERN "CRAB"

T.ME/CRYPTOZ

67

As we reach the final page of this trading education ebook, I want to extend my heartfelt gratitude to each and every one of you for embarking on this educational journey with us. It has been a pleasure to be your guide through the complex world of trading, and I hope you've found the information

contained within these pages both informative and valuable.
Trading can be an exciting and potentially lucrative endeavor, but it's essential to remember that it also carries risks. The knowledge you've gained here is a valuable tool, but it should always be used responsibly. None of the information in this ebook constitutes financial advice, and it's crucial to consult with a qualified financial advisor or professional before making any trading decisions.

Remember, successful trading is not about getting rich overnight. It's about continuous learning, discipline, risk management, and the ability to adapt to changing market conditions. The journey to becoming a skilled trader is ongoing, and I encourage you to stay curious, stay informed, and never stop learning.

Whether you are just starting or have been trading for years, I hope you find success and fulfillment in your trading endeavors. Always approach the markets with caution and respect for the potential risks involved, and may your journey be filled with profitable opportunities and valuable lessons.
Thank you once again for choosing to learn with us. I wish you all the best in your trading adventures, and may your financial goals and dreams become a reality.

Happy Trading and Take Care!

CRYPTOZ

T.ME/CRYPTOZ

info@cryptoz.media

Printed in Great Britain
by Amazon